HOWARD
THURMAN

MODERN SPIRITUAL MASTERS
Robert Ellsberg, Series Editor

Already published:

Dietrich Bonhoeffer (edited by Robert Coles)
Simone Weil (edited by Eric O. Springsted)
Henri Nouwen (edited by Robert A. Jonas)
Pierre Teilhard de Chardin (edited by Ursula King)
Anthony de Mello (edited by William Dych, S.J.)
Charles de Foucauld (edited by Robert Ellsberg)
Oscar Romero (by Marie Dennis, Rennie Golden,
    and Scott Wright)
Eberhard Arnold (edited by Johann Christoph Arnold)
Thomas Merton (edited by Christine M. Bochen)
Thich Nhat Hanh (edited by Robert Ellsberg)
Rufus Jones (edited by Kerry Walters)
Mother Teresa (edited by Jean Maalouf)
Edith Stein (edited by John Sullivan, O.C.D.)
John Main (edited by Laurence Freeman)
Mohandas Gandhi (edited by John Dear)
Mother Maria Skobtsova (introduction by Jim Forest)
Evelyn Underhill (edited by Emilie Griffin)
St. Thérèse of Lisieux (edited by Mary Frohlich)
Flannery O'Connor (edited by Robert Ellsberg)
Clarence Jordan (edited by Joyce Hollyday)
G. K. Chesterton (edited by William Griffin)
Alfred Delp, SJ (introduction by Thomas Merton)
Bede Griffiths (edited by Thomas Matus)
Karl Rahner (edited by Philip Endean)
Sadhu Sundar Singh (edited by Charles E. Moore)
Pedro Arrupe (edited by Kevin F. Burke, S.J.)
Romano Guardini (edited by Robert A. Krieg)
Albert Schweitzer (edited by James Brabazon)
Caryll Houselander (edited by Wendy M. Wright)
Brother Roger of Taizé (edited by Marcello Fidanzio)
Dorothee Soelle (edited by Dianne L. Oliver)
Leo Tolstoy (edited by Charles E. Moore)

MODERN SPIRITUAL MASTERS SERIES

HOWARD THURMAN

Essential Writings

Selected with an Introduction by

LUTHER E. SMITH, JR.

ORBIS BOOKS

Maryknoll, New York 10545

Founded in 1970, Orbis Books endeavors to publish works that enlighten the mind, nourish the spirit, and challenge the conscience. The publishing arm of the Maryknoll Fathers and Brothers, Orbis seeks to explore the global dimensions of the Christian faith and mission, to invite dialogue with diverse cultures and religious traditions, and to serve the cause of reconciliation and peace. The books published reflect the views of their authors and do not represent the official position of the Maryknoll Society. To learn more about Maryknoll and Orbis Books, please visit our website at www.maryknoll.org.

Library of Congress Cataloging-in-Publication Data

Thurman, Howard, 1899–1981.
    [Selections. 2006]
    Howard Thurman : essential writings / selected with an Introduction by Luther E. Smith, Jr.
      p. cm. – (Modern spiritual masters series)
    ISBN-13: 978-1-57075-670-2 (pbk.)
    ISBN-10: 1-57075-670-8
    1. Theology. 2. Baptists – Doctrines. I. Smith, Luther E. II. Title.
III. Series.
BX6447.T48 2006
230′.044 – dc22

                                      2006014547

Contents

Sources 7

Preface 9

Introduction:
THE CALL TO PROPHETIC SPIRITUALITY 13

1. RELIGIOUS EXPERIENCE: ENCOUNTERING GOD 35
   Deep Calls unto Deep 37
   Spiritual Disciplines 45
   The Exemplary Jesus 65
   The Church's Challenge 77
   Reason for Hope 81

2. THE HUNGER FOR COMMUNITY 88
   The Nature of Nature 90
   Community as Crucible 96
   The Hounds of Hell 101
   Race as Crisis 106
   Jesus and the Love-Ethic 117
   Nonviolence and Reconciling Community 121

3. THE AUTHENTIC SELF 129
   Centered in God 131
   The Meaning of Self 137
   Living as a Free Person 146
   At Home in Community 157
   Near Journey's End 162
   Renewal of the Self 167

Sources

The Centering Moment (New York: Harper & Row, 1969; Richmond, IN: Friends United Press, 1980).

The Creative Encounter (New York: Harper & Row, 1954; Richmond, IN: Friends United Press, 1972).

Deep Is the Hunger (New York: Harper & Row, 1951; Richmond, IN: Friends United Press, 1973).

Deep River (Mills College, CA: Eucalyptus Press, 1945; revised edition New York: Harper & Row, 1955) and *The Negro Spiritual Speaks of Life and Death* (New York: Harper & Brothers, 1947). Single volume of the two books (Richmond, IN: Friends United Press, 1975).

Disciplines of the Spirit (New York: Harper & Row, 1963; Richmond, IN: Friends United Press, 1977).

The Inward Journey (New York: Harper & Row, 1961; Richmond, IN: Friends United Press, 1971).

Jesus and the Disinherited (Nashville: Abingdon, 1949; Richmond, IN: Friends United Press, 1981; Boston: Beacon Press, 1996).

The Luminous Darkness (New York: Harper & Row, 1965; Richmond, IN: Friends United Press, 1989).

Meditations of the Heart (New York: Harper & Row, 1953; Richmond, IN: Friends United Press, 1976; Boston: Beacon Press, 1999).

The Mood of Christmas (New York: Harper & Row, 1973; Richmond, IN: Friends United Press, 1985).

Mysticism and the Experience of Love (Wallingford, PA: Pendle Hill Pamphlet 115, 1961).

The Search for Common Ground (New York: Harper & Row, 1971; Richmond, IN: Friends United Press, 1986).

Temptations of Jesus: Five Sermons (San Francisco: Lawton Kennedy, 1962; Richmond, IN: Friends United Press, 1978).

With Head and Heart: The Autobiography of Howard Thurman (New York: Harcourt Brace and Company, 1979).

Preface

Memory and Hope

Our ability to live creatively in the future relies upon our being instructed by the creative impulses of the past. This is one of the reasons why people of faith read the narratives of their sacred texts and their religious histories. This heritage often inspires; it always teaches. Current challenges have roots that stretch across the centuries. Ancient wisdom yearns to speak anew to every era. Again and again, sacred texts tell us to "remember." The past is source and resource for becoming a people of hope. If we remember rightly, no one should have to live as an orphan from the past.

Howard Thurman was a prophetic witness whose life and writings offer us needed insights for our times and the years ahead. In his eighty-one years (1899–1981), Thurman lived during a period of dramatic changes in the United States and the world. Throughout his childhood, the experience of slavery was still fresh in the memory and behaviors of African Americans. Discrimination and segregation were legal for most of Thurman's life. The Great Depression devastated lives and threatened to breed social chaos. Colonialism was overthrown throughout most of the world. Two World Wars, the Korean War, the Vietnam War, and the Cold War mobilized and spent the energies of the nation. And the world was introduced to nuclear weapons as a means to end war and eliminate life as we know it. Thurman not only lived during this time; his speaking, writings, and service addressed the issues of his time. He believed the thriving of the human spirit required attentiveness to the realities of the social order. Spiritual wholeness and social wholeness are interrelated.

During his lifetime, Howard Thurman received considerable recognition for his contributions. He had thousands of speaking invitations, was awarded numerous honorary degrees, was listed in two national magazines as one of the greatest preachers in the United States, and was made an honorary canon of the Cathedral Church of St. John the Divine in New York City.

As I write, a statue of Howard Thurman is being sculpted for dedication and display in the National Cathedral in Washington, DC. Courses are taught on his thought in seminaries. Articles on him appear in the *Dictionary of Pastoral Care and Counseling,* the *Dictionary of Biblical Interpretation,* and the *Dictionary of Modern American Philosophers.* And scholars have written whole books on his thought and contributions.

A major development for the interpretation of Thurman's life and significance is the Howard Thurman Papers Project. His private correspondence, administrative reports, and lesser known publications will be available in three annotated volumes. The extent of the documents collected for review and publication makes this the second largest papers project on an African American — second only to the Martin Luther King Jr. Papers Project. Such a project indicates Thurman's historical significance and provides new materials for comprehending his legacy.

But even with all the recognition given to Howard Thurman during his lifetime and after, there is a surprisingly large number of readers in the literature of spirituality who are not familiar with him. Many of these persons have read quotes of Thurman in books, church bulletins, and magazines; or they have heard references to Thurman in sermons and lectures. But they have not known where to start reading in order to be introduced to his thinking. This Orbis publication on Thurman provides readers a place to meet Thurman and hear the major themes of his prophetic spirituality. Such a place of meeting and hearing will hopefully create new memories for readers to live creatively and faithfully into the future.

A Word about Words

Howard Thurman's use of male nouns (e.g., man, brother, mankind) and pronouns (e.g., he, his) for references to males and females reflects the convention of his time. I realize that such usage is difficult if not offensive to many contemporary readers. Personally, whenever I quote Thurman in my public speaking, I edit the language so that the inclusive intent of Thurman's message is heard. However, the Thurman Estate has requested that publications of his writing be quoted as written. The original language is therefore preserved in this collection.

Thurman's life bears witness to gender equality. Women were colleagues and sources of authority. Olive Schreiner, the nineteenth-century novelist and advocate for women's rights, was the only person whose collected writings Thurman edited for a book publication (*A Track to the Water's Edge: The Olive Schreiner Reader*). He encouraged women in ministry long before most denominations recognized their gifts. Over the years, he demonstrated integrity and respect for women in formal and informal relationships. His marriage to Sue Bailey Thurman was a partnership of mutual support and affirmation. In saying this, my intent is to help the reader know that Thurman's heart and life were a true expression of what "inclusive language" symbolizes to many in today's culture.

I also believe that we must be careful in our expectations that writing from a previous era conform to current sensitivities. Such an expectation can alienate us from history. Perhaps hearing persons in the voices of their time and culture is a gift we must discipline ourselves to receive. All of us are speaking and writing with language that may be offensive to future generations. Whatever our sensibilities about language, I hope they do not become an obstacle to our ability to hear the "sound of the genuine" in another. May our hearts be humbled to embrace the wisdom that comes in any language that is not our own.

Acknowledgments

I so appreciate Robert Ellsberg of Orbis Books for the invitation to be the editor for this book. His patience and support provided the time needed to give myself fully to this project. Olive Thurman Wong's embrace of the project and her approval for use of Howard Thurman's writings were essential to even considering the possibility of this book. Carmen Armstrong, Brenda Gresham, Anna Hall, and Fred Kim helped in typing the selected Thurman writings. And my wife, Helen Pearson Smith, encouraged me and gave wise counsel throughout every phase of this work. My sense of indebtedness is exceeded only by my gratitude for such blessings.

Introduction

The Call to Prophetic Spirituality

The Vocation of Time and Place

Near the end of his senior year at Rochester Theological Seminary, Howard Thurman met with one of his theological mentors — Professor George Cross. The meeting had a defining moment when Dr. Cross advised Thurman on his vocational direction. Thurman recalls:

> He [Cross] was smiling and enthusiastic as I told him my plans. Presently his demeanor became sober, even grave. What followed astounded me. He told me that I had superior gifts and that he felt it probable that I would be able to make an original contribution to the spiritual life of the times. That said, he went to the heart of his concern. "You are a very sensitive Negro man," he said, "and doubtless feel under great obligation to put all the weight of your mind and spirit at the disposal of the struggle of your own people for full citizenship. But let me remind you that all social questions are transitory in nature and it would be a terrible waste for you to limit your creative energy to the solution of the race problem, however insistent its nature. Give yourself to the timeless issues of the human spirit," he advised. When I did not reply, he said, "Perhaps I have no right to say this to you because as a white man I can never know what it is to be in your situation." I pondered the meaning of his words, and wondered what kind of response I could make to this man who did not know that

a man and his black skin must face the "timeless issues of the human spirit" together.[1]

Thurman's concluding assertion characterizes his approach to spirituality: "social questions" are integral to the spiritual life. This conviction not only guided his personal spiritual quest; it also led Thurman to pioneer spiritual insights that would have a profound influence on individuals, the church, and society.

Repeatedly, Thurman asks, "How can I believe that life has meaning if I do not believe that my own life has meaning?" Thurman poses this question/affirmation to stress how one's autobiography is connected to spirituality. Whatever one seeks to discover about the meaning of life in general must take into consideration how such meaning is found in one's own life. Thurman's life is therefore a vital source for understanding his prophetic spirituality.

Born in Daytona, Florida, in 1899, Howard Thurman knew nurture, struggle, and heartache in his childhood. He and his two sisters had loving parents. When he was seven, however, their father died. This left the major responsibility for raising them on their mother and maternal grandmother. Beyond the immediate family, Thurman refers to his church, neighborhood, and experiences with nature (especially a particular oak tree, the Halifax River, the woods, nightfall, and the Atlantic Ocean) as sources of stability and reassurance in what was often a hostile racial environment.

His grandmother, even more than his mother (who spent long hours as a domestic worker in the homes of white people), took the primary parental role. She was born a slave. Even though she could neither read nor write, she insisted that Thurman excel in his education. He marveled in her strength of character and religious sensibility. Later in his life he would declare:

> I learned more, for instance, about the genius of the reli-
> gion of Jesus from my grandmother than from all the men
> who taught me all...the Greek and all the rest of it. Be-
> cause she moved inside the experience [of the religion of
> Jesus] and lived out of that kind of center.[2]

Thurman believed that she embodied Christian faith. He also
admired her ability to challenge church officials who chose their
church protocols over caring for the needs of her family. In his
grandmother he saw a survivor of slavery who exhibited moral
authority and religious integrity. Throughout his life, Thurman
continually referred to her as a source of wisdom and assurance.

The support and determination of his family were essential to
his pursuit of an education. The racial discrimination policies
of Daytona prevented black youth from qualifying for a high
school education. The public school system failed to offer the
eighth grade for black students; and with the inability to complete the eighth grade, these students did not qualify for high
school. Thurman's elementary school principal volunteered to
tutor him so that Thurman could pass the eighth grade equiv-
alency examination. After passing the examination, Thurman
pursued his secondary education at the Florida Baptist Academy
in Jacksonville, Florida — a private church-supported school for
black students. Although his mother and grandmother did not
have the money to pay for his education, they encouraged him
to pursue an education. With support from a cousin during his
first year of school and hard work at various jobs throughout
his high school career, Thurman covered his educational and
living expenses.

He excelled at Florida Baptist Academy and graduated as
the valedictorian of his class. This honor earned him a tui-
tion scholarship at Morehouse College in Atlanta, Georgia.
At Morehouse, Thurman was on the debate team, edited the
school's literary magazine, and was heavily involved in the

campus YMCA. His academic performance was exceptional. Another indicator of his intellectual passion, however, is that as a senior student he read every book in the Morehouse library. One of the most important influences of the Morehouse ethos was the affirmation he felt as a black man. The students were often addressed by faculty as "Mister (last name)" and "young gentlemen." Morehouse instilled pride, dignity, and confidence about being a black man in a society that belittled black worth. In 1923, Thurman graduated as valedictorian and received his bachelor of arts degree from Morehouse with a major in economics.

He was accepted at Rochester Theological Seminary in Rochester, New York, where he pursued preparation for Christian ministry. The seminary's policy was to enroll no more than two black students a year. Consequently, for the first time in Thurman's life, his primary academic and living community was predominantly white. He found himself challenged by the notion that he had an ethical responsibility to these white persons. Before this time, relationships with white persons were formal matters determined by the laws and customs of segregation. Physical survival was often the main objective in such relationships. Now Thurman found himself in situations of social intimacy that made new demands on his understanding of who inhabited his ethical world. Both his image of community and his theological boundaries expanded at Rochester. Personal relationships and critical theological reflection led him to pursue truth beyond the confines of convention and dogma.

Thurman graduated with a bachelor of divinity degree from Rochester in 1926. He married Kate Kelley and became the pastor of Mount Zion Baptist Church in Oberlin, Ohio. Mount Zion was a black Baptist congregation whose membership primarily came from Oberlin citizens. During Thurman's pastorate, an increasing number of local college students attended the church. Here he cultivated his preaching style, experimented with liturgy, taught religious education courses, and entered into situations of celebration and tragedy that demanded his pastoral skills. Thurman labored to make the insights of his seminary education available to his congregation. He implemented creative ideas that established his determination to be a caring leader who honored his members' capacity for spiritual growth. And he experienced the membership and their life situations as mentors for his personal and professional growth.

Transformations abounded for him in Oberlin. Thurman coped with his tendencies of shyness and being a private person. He began postgraduate study with Old and New Testament scholars. A daughter was born. His religious experiences deepened and defined the directions of his spiritual and vocational formation. During Sunday morning worship services, the visitors were racially diverse — though only black visitors joined the church. And he explored religious community within a diverse gathering. Regarding this last transformation, Thurman writes:

> One afternoon a Chinese gentleman came to see me. I had seen him in church each Sunday morning for many weeks. Always he slipped away quietly without speaking to anyone. Now he introduced himself, saying that he was returning to China and wanted to tell me good-bye and express his appreciation for the experience of worshipping with us each Sunday morning. "When I close my eyes and listen with my spirit I am in my Buddhist temple experiencing the renewing of my own spirit." I knew then what I had only sensed before. The barriers were crumbling. I was breaking new ground. Yet it would be many years before I would fully understand the nature of the breakthrough.[3]

Among the transformations was the health of his wife: Kate had tuberculosis. In 1928, her doctors recommended that moving to a milder climate would increase her chances of recovery. She and their daughter, Olive, moved to LaGrange, Georgia, where her family assisted in the care of Kate and their daughter.

The last Oberlin transformation occurred when Thurman resigned from the church and in January 1929 began a semester of directed study at Haverford College with Quaker mystic, scholar, and social activist Rufus Jones. Jones guided Thurman's first extensive formal study of mysticism. Thurman described his time with Jones as "a watershed from which flowed much of the thought and endeavor to which I was to commit the rest of my working life."[4] More specifically Thurman says,

> He gave to me confidence in the insight that the religion of the inner life could deal with the empirical experience of man without retreating from the demands of such experience. To state what I mean categorically, the religion of the inner life at its best is life affirming rather than life denying and must forever be involved in the Master's instruction, "Be ye perfect, even as your heavenly father is perfect."[5]

For Thurman, "empirical experience" would entail all the glorious and horrible realities of living. If he had lingering doubts about his resistance to Dr. George Cross's advice to avoid "social questions," the time with Jones must have resolved them.

In the fall 1929, Howard Thurman returned to Atlanta to teach religion and philosophy at Morehouse and to teach the Bible and serve as religious advisor to students and faculty at Spelman College (which is adjacent to Morehouse). He immediately had responsibility for chapel services at Spelman and later had responsibility for all the daily chapel services at Morehouse. These positions enabled him to pursue his passion for working with college students. Thurman had numerous speaking engagements at college campuses and student conferences. In addition, he was very active in organizations devoted to cultivating leadership among college students — especially the YMCA. The move to Atlanta also provided him a job that was close to his ill wife — whom he soon moved to Atlanta.

Kate Kelley Thurman died in December 1930. Her death was devastating to Thurman. In an effort to deal with his physical and emotional exhaustion, he traveled to Europe in the summer of 1931 for an extended period of rest and reflection. Upon returning to Morehouse and Spelman, he met Sue Bailey, a former friend, and by June 1932 they were married. Throughout the rest of his life, Thurman attributed his personal and professional growth to his partnership with Sue Bailey Thurman.

A few months after their marriage, he joined the faculty of Howard University's School of Religion as professor of Christian Theology. Along with classroom teaching, he chaired the university's Committee on Religious Life. His role overseeing matters related to the chapel and religious programs later led to his being appointed dean of the university's Rankin Chapel. Thurman continued to have a vigorous speaking schedule across the nation, and he remained active with organizations focused on developing college student leadership. In 1933, Sue Bailey Thurman gave birth to their daughter, Anne.

In the fall of 1935, Sue Bailey Thurman and Howard Thurman, with another African American couple, became the delegation for a six-month "Pilgrimage of Friendship" sponsored by the World Student Christian Federation and the National YMCA and YWCA International Committee. The delegation traveled to India, Burma, and Ceylon, interpreting the black experience in the United States and relating their understanding of the meaning of the Christian faith to this experience. Thurman continually found himself explaining why the Christian faith

was unable to eliminate the injustices of segregation and discrimination. The many questions and challenges required him
to distinguish between the inclusive love of the religion of Jesus
and culture-dominated expressions of Christianity. He was also
keenly aware that he could not point to any churches in the
United States that were exemplary, in membership and leadership, in overcoming the racial divide. At Khyber Pass, looking
into Afghanistan, he had a vision that his life must be given
to a commitment that responded to questions about the church
and race.

The high point of the pilgrimage was a meeting that he, Sue
Bailey Thurman, and one other member of the delegation had
with Mohandas K. Gandhi. They were the first African Americans to meet with Gandhi, and they discovered his eagerness to
find out about the plight of black people in the United States.
Most of the session was consumed with Gandhi's questions and
their replies. Near the end, the Thurmans invited Gandhi to
come to the United States to address the race issue, but he felt
that his struggle in India had to be won before he could offer
counsel elsewhere.

When Thurman returned to the United States, he traveled
throughout the country speaking about his time with Gandhi
and the relevance of nonviolent resistance as a means for addressing racial injustices. Newspaper clippings from that time
indicate that Thurman stood on the national stage as a prophetic messenger for social transformation. Other black leaders
were inspired to meet with Gandhi: Mordecai Johnson (then
president of Howard University) and Benjamin E. Mays (then
dean of Howard University's School of Religion). Mordecai
Johnson also spoke extensively about his time with Gandhi
and is said to have inspired Martin Luther King Jr.'s interest
in Gandhi. Directly and indirectly, Thurman was the messenger for connecting the spiritual methods of India's struggle for

independence to the need for a spiritually based nonviolent movement to transform racial injustices in the United States.

He also continued to teach this message and its implications in his classes at Howard University. James Farmer, who would become a founder of the Committee for Racial Equality (CORE), later to be called the Congress for Racial Equality, was a seminary student in Thurman's class. He considered Thurman to be a favorite teacher, who helped him in forming a nonviolent ethic and in becoming socially active. Other civil rights activists gave similar testimony to Thurman's influence in their lives.

As dean of Rankin Chapel, Howard Thurman crafted liturgies that introduced dance and other artistic expressions to university worship. He brought major religious, educational, and social leaders to the campus as speakers for worship services and special programs. He involved Howard University in exchange programs with other colleges in ways that pioneered the integration of these schools. And he was constantly in demand to speak at college campuses, student conferences, church services, community events, and meetings of peace organizations.

Certainly, the substance of Thurman's messages was cause for his appeal as a speaker. Audiences connected to his emphases on personal worth, God's immediacy, the reality of community, and other themes of religious commitment. He spoke perspectives that resonated with many traditional understandings of the self, community, and God. He also articulated ideas that stretched listeners beyond familiar concepts of Jesus, God's dream for community, the religious significance of ordinary encounters, and social issues. The Bible was a major source of authority for his public speaking. His life experience, literature, biography, philosophy, science, social studies research, and history were also prominent sources of authority. In utilizing these various sources, Thurman conveyed that all of life was material for the spiritual quest.

His speaking style captivated audiences. He was a master in the use of silence. At times, he would be so overwhelmed by an understanding that he seemed to be in a trance. Humor and storytelling were the staples of a Thurman speech. As he talked about the crises, brutalities, discoveries, and joys in his own life, listeners felt invited into the intimacy of his heart. And messages usually challenged his audience to do whatever was necessary to embrace life as fully as God intended. A common conclusion from persons was that "listening to Howard Thurman is a religious experience."

In 1944, with his prominent position at Howard University, his popularity as a national speaker, and his reputation as religious leader, many persons were surprised to hear that Howard Thurman had decided to join a small group of persons who were forming an interracial and intercultural church fellowship in San Francisco. Thurman, however, perceived their invitation as the opportunity to fulfill his Khyber Pass vision regarding race and the church.

With Thurman's arrival, the organization of the church accelerated and the membership increased dramatically. The name became the Church for the Fellowship of All Peoples — also known as Fellowship Church. Considerable national press was given to its founding and work as the first interracial and intercultural church, in both membership and leadership, in the United States. About 60 percent of the membership was Euro-Americans, 35 percent African Americans, and 5 percent had a heritage that was either Chinese, Japanese, or of other ethnic groups. In addition to resident members, Fellowship Church had members-at-large. This latter group comprised persons who embraced the goals and commitment of the church, but who lived far from San Francisco. The official status of member-at-large indicated a deeper commitment and level of affiliation than those who only made financial contributions to Fellowship

Church. Among the members-at-large were Eleanor Roosevelt and Mary McCloud Bethune.

Fellowship Church inspired and informed the birth of other interracial churches throughout the nation. And denominational organizations would reference Fellowship Church as an example for their congregations and the establishment of new churches. In addition to innovative programs and the experience of diversity for its members, Fellowship Church became the example of a diverse Christian fellowship for others. For Thurman, it tested the ability of the Christian faith to overcome culturally imposed walls between people. Thurman summarizes the significance of the church:

> There has not been a single day since the beginning of the church that I have not been moved by its spirit. It was not the unique essence of any particular creed or faith; it was timeless and time-bound, the idiom of all creeds and totally contained in none, the authentic accent of every gospel but limited to none, the growing edge that marks the boundaries of all that destroys and plunders and lays waste. For a breathless moment in time, a little group of diverse peoples was caught up in a dream as old as life and as new as a hope that just emerges on the horizon of becoming man.[6]

While at Fellowship Church, Thurman assumed this would be the last position of his professional career. The church and its work were challenging, expanding, and fulfilling. The invitation to become Boston University's dean of Marsh Chapel and professor of Spiritual Resources and Disciplines felt like an opportunity to advance the Fellowship Church model. The diversity of Boston University and its surrounding area were promising features of the invitation. Rather than being a complete break from Fellowship Church, Thurman envisioned his call to Marsh Chapel as an opportunity to replicate and further disseminate the Fellowship Church model.

The Marsh Chapel years (1953–63) were a creative and productive time. Just before his arrival at Boston University, a poll taken by the popular *Life* magazine identified Thurman as one of the twelve greatest preachers in the United States. A year later, *Ebony* magazine would name him one of the "ten greatest Negro preachers in America." His preaching was a major factor for reinvigorating Marsh Chapel services. As mentioned earlier, the life of the mind, with all the attendant resources of history, literature, science, and scholarly interpretations of biblical texts, was emphasized in his sermons along with the affective, intuitive, and devotional dimensions of the heart. But worship involved more than his preaching. Sunday morning services also reflected Thurman's belief in the arts as a means of religious experience. The sanctuary was usually full, and a congregation of consistent and active participation in ministries formed. During his last seven years at the university, he had a weekly television program on which he gave religious meditations. Thurman's ministry was far-reaching. With a television audience, his popularity as a teacher in the classroom, the national attention given to his leadership at Marsh Chapel, the publication of his books, and the endless invitations to preach and lecture, Thurman was a prominent religious leader.

In 1963, Marsh Chapel "membership" did not exist. However, a strong sense of commitment to Marsh Chapel led many persons to want a formal membership status. They also recommended new structures of programming and decision-making for the chapel. The university's board of trustees concluded that their recommendations for new structures and membership would redefine the chapel in ways that diminished the university's authority over it. Thurman was disappointed with the trustees' decision and resigned the position of dean. He became minister-at-large — a position that released him from administrative responsibilities and allowed him to be more available for speaking engagements and personal travel.

After his retirement in 1965, Thurman founded the Howard Thurman Educational Trust and moved to San Francisco. The Trust provided need-based financial assistance to college students (particularly at black colleges), supported programs that fostered intercultural understanding, archived his professional papers and materials, and sponsored seminars on the spiritual life. Throughout his remaining years, he directed the trust, published, and spoke extensively. He died on April 11, 1981, at his home in San Francisco.

Texts of Context

Even though he wrote over twenty books and numerous articles, Thurman insisted "my craft remains the spoken word." The preceding biographical profile notes that he was a popular, inspirational, and influential speaker. His writing also gives powerful testimony to his spirituality. Dr. George Cross's counsel to him suggested that "the timeless issues of the human spirit" and "social questions" are separate realities. In Thurman's writing, each may have its moment for concentrated analysis and reflection, but they are never separated. Intense attention to one results in insights and energy for intense attention to the other.

Thurman's social analysis and theology are based on understanding the relationship of the *particular* to the *universal*. Thurman believes that a *particular* contains the *universal,* and the universal is composed of particulars. A proper understanding of the worth and significance of particulars is essential to realizing God's dream for universal community. If a particular race, ethnicity, gender, or nation is defined as the sole bearer of the universal, the conditions are established for domination, oppression, and perhaps genocide. Particulars must be valued as bearers of the universal, but no particular can claim to be the sole proprietary expression of the universal.

In two of Thurman's early books, *Deep River* (1945) and *The Negro Spiritual Speaks of Life and Death* (1947), he examines his religious heritage through the spirituals of black slaves. Thurman is convinced that the slaves' particularity is a source of wisdom, instruction, and truth. Their slave status does not disqualify them from being bearers of universal meaning. In his interpretation of their spirituals he concludes:

> And this is the miracle of their achievement causing them to take their place alongside the great creative religious thinkers of the human race. They made a worthless life, the life of chattel property, a mere thing, a body, *worth living!*[7]

In fact, for Thurman, their particularity provides a distinctive insight about the power of faith under the most horrendous life-denying conditions. As slaves, their professions of faith have the credibility of being forged under conditions that raise searing questions about God's loving presence. They sing universal truths about the capacity to know God's love despite suffering and death. Thurman's examination of the slave songs is an exercise that affirms his own particularity. He discovers within his particular heritage that which is a profound and creative testimony to the universal human spirit.

Another early book of Thurman's is *Jesus and the Disinherited* (1949). This ever popular book (perhaps the most seminal of his publications) interprets the ministry of Jesus as a resource for resolving contemporary racial crises. The most quoted phrase from the book is the generative question: "What, then, is the word of the religion of Jesus to those who stand with their backs against the wall?" A vivid image is created. We see a people driven by powerful forces to a place where retreat is no longer possible. To move forward means battle with an enemy whose strength has pushed them to a wall of no retreat. To remain means to feel the constant pressure of the enemy who seeks to crush them against the wall. In this situation of survival, does Jesus (or as Thurman asks, "the religion of Jesus") offer any answers that help the disinherited in this predicament of no exit?

He begins by assessing Jesus' context of crisis. Thurman concludes that the disinherited of his own time live under conditions that are analogous to those of Jesus. He interprets Jesus as a poor man who is a member of an oppressed people suffering from Roman governance. This conclusion is critical to Thurman, for he believes that only those who have experienced standing with their backs against the wall can offer inspiration and hope to the disinherited. Jesus knows fully the reality of the "wall."

Thurman's question regarding the religion of Jesus for the disinherited is not academic. He is deeply invested in the question because Thurman himself is one of the disinherited. He writes:

> The striking similarity between the social position of Jesus in Palestine and that of the vast majority of American Negroes is obvious to anyone who tarries long over the facts. We are dealing here with conditions that produce essentially the same psychology.[8]

The generating question could be recast to reflect Thurman's personal investment: "What does the religion of Jesus have to say to *me* (Howard Thurman) and my people, who stand with *our* backs against the wall?"

Jesus and the Disinherited not only clarifies the social realities and spiritual challenges; it gives the disinherited a sense of option for their circumstances. Freedom, for Thurman, is contingent on a sense of option. Slavery is the loss of options or, more specifically, the loss of options that enable the expression of one's God-given identity. The "wall" is a barricade for enslavement. However, giving all of one's energies to addressing the wall misreads the reality. The disinherited are dealing with an enemy who will pursue them to another wall even if they should escape the immediate one. Condemning the wall or deftly fleeing the conflict are not solutions.

Thurman suggests an option that gives the disinherited the initiative in such situations. This option declares their humanity, power, and freedom. The option is to *love the enemy*. The enemy does not control the initiative to love. The oppressed are not dependent on the generosity or the brutality of the oppressor for this expression of freedom. Those with their backs against the wall can choose to respond faithfully as God has required. They exercise the freedom to love. Enemies cannot crush and walls cannot contain this God-given initiative.

This may explain why Martin Luther King Jr. carried *Jesus and the Disinherited* with him during the Montgomery boycott. This may explain why civil rights activists Kelly Miller Smith, James Bevel, James Lawson, Otis Moss, C. T. Vivian, and John Lewis read *Jesus and the Disinherited* as they prepared for social protest. This may explain why people who will never be identified as principal actors in social movements have found this book to embolden their spiritual resources for personal and social struggle. This may explain why James Cone identifies *Jesus and the Disinherited* as an influential book for his development of a black theology of liberation.

For almost sixty years, *Jesus and the Disinherited* has remained an inspiring text for engaging contemporary issues of social conflict. Readers may gravitate to different aspects of Thurman's argument and emerge with their distinctive sense of assurance and empowerment. Clearly, those with their backs against the wall have read within its pages a description of their plight and their hope for good news. Thurman has inspired such readers to exclaim (paraphrasing the black spiritual), "Somebody knows the trouble we've seen. Glory, hallelujah!"

Howard Thurman's *The Luminous Darkness: A Personal Interpretation of the Anatomy of Segregation and the Ground of Hope* is his only other book fully devoted to the issues of race and Christian faith. The complete corpus of his publications makes clear that he does not reduce the "timeless issues of the human spirit" to addressing race. Early in his career, Thurman resisted invitations to speak only on race. He understood himself as focusing on the meaning of religion. This meaning included race, but it neither required him nor did it limit him to address racial topics.

Within all of his writing, social contexts are important for understanding and practicing spirituality. A multitude of personal, interpersonal, and social issues, however, are creating the climate of nurture or abuse in social contexts. Thurman believes that the personality is a gift of God that enables individuals to interact creatively with social realities. Through personality one interprets meaning and derives purpose for living. Individuals come to know their worth as children of God, and their response-ability to life as persons of faith, when they have a proper sense of self. These matters of meaning, purpose, worth, and responsibility rely upon one's attentiveness to one's self. So Thurman expends considerable writing on the spiritual practices that prepare the personality to discern what contributes to and what diminishes a proper sense of self.

His books cover a wide range of religious concerns such as the importance of waiting, loneliness, forgiveness, celebration, hospitality, discernment, and attentiveness. *Meditations for Apostles of Sensitiveness* (1947), *Deep Is the Hunger* (1951), *Meditations of the Heart* (1953), *The Inward Journey* (1961), and *The Mood of Christmas* (1973) are books of his poetry and meditations. *The Centering Moment* (1969) is a book of his prayers that preceded his sermons at Marsh Chapel. *The Creative Encounter* (1954) and *Mysticism and the Experience of Love* (1961) discuss the relationship of religious experience to social witness. *The Greatest of These* (1944) and *The Temptations of Jesus* (1962) are devotional reflections upon New Testament texts. *The Growing Edge* (1956) is a book of his sermons. *Footprints of a Dream* (1959) and *The First Footprints* (1975) tell the story of Fellowship Church. *Disciplines of the Spirit* (1963) examines the significance of commitment, growth, prayer, suffering, and reconciliation as disciplines that ready us for religious experience and enable us to live the implications of that experience. *The Search for Common Ground* (1971) is Thurman's investigation of the urge for community as found in myths, biology, utopian ideals, and human consciousness. And *With Head and Heart: The Autobiography of Howard Thurman* (1979) gives a reader great insight into how his personal history shapes his spirituality.

The major themes in Howard Thurman's spirituality are the significance of religious experience, the hunger for community, and the realization of a true sense of self. Within each of these themes, a proper understanding of particularity and universality is crucial. Earlier discussion focused on the breakdown in community when particular and universal dimensions of social relationships are distorted. Hegemony, oppression, and injustice become the customs and laws. Such a breakdown leads to a crisis for experiencing community and a sense of self as God intends.

This conviction also applies to Thurman's perspective on Christianity in relationship to other religions. He believes Christianity is a particular religious expression that should not lay claim to being *the* universal expression of religion. Thurman insists that Christian identity can be based on knowing Jesus as Friend and Lord without turning Jesus Christ into the only way to God.

In sermons, Thurman often quoted from other religious traditions. Hindu mystics, Jainism, Buddha, Lao Tzu, and Greek philosophers were the subjects of a sermon series. The membership statement of Fellowship Church reflected this appreciation of other religions as sources of spiritual and moral authority:

> I affirm my need for a growing understanding of all men as sons of God, and I seek after a vital experience of God as revealed in Jesus of Nazareth and other great religious spirits whose fellowship with God was the foundation of their fellowship with man.
>
> I desire to share in the spiritual growth and ethical awareness of men and women of varied national cultural, racial, and creedal heritage united in a religious fellowship.[9]

To be clear, this is not forsaking Christianity as one's own particularity into which one desires to live, move, and have one's being. Thurman believes one can be thoroughly Christian without perceiving oneself to be superior to other religions. This is not being generous; it is to acknowledge God's presence and revelation in other particularities. Perhaps the spiritual virtue most related to such a conviction is humility. If one cannot limit God's freedom to be where God will be, and if one cannot claim to exhaustively know God's will among a people, then one's spirit is more faithful and nourished through humility and reverence than through certainty and judgment.

An exploration into Thurman's spirituality may prove important beyond understanding the creative impulses of his thinking and witness during his time and place. In addition to his rich legacy of influence on the civil rights movement, ecclesiology, interpreting Jesus, preaching, and spiritual practices, Thurman gives vital perspectives and approaches for creative community in our increasingly pluralistic societies. His emphasis on the embrace of one's own particularity and the particularities of others relates to matters of race, ethnicity, culture, gender, sexual orientation, nationality, and faith. Any hope for our living together peacefully in diverse communities may depend on how his message is implemented as a resource for this endeavor.

Thurman is too wise to assert a concept of "anything goes." He relies upon spiritual disciplines to tutor our spiritual discernment so that both the familiar and the strange are understood in light of the desires of God's heart. There are life-affirming and life-destroying impulses within both the familiar and the strange. A spirituality for the future must help each person discern the challenges within self and with neighbors. Discipline and discernment are essential practices in facing the barrage of choices that come with increased pluralism.

For Thurman, this means total surrender to God and living life in the joy of trusting God. Only God can provide the security and confidence to face these challenges. Without trust in God, we are left to our fears, prejudices, ambitions, weapons, and obsessions with certainty (even in our theological constructions). With trust in God, life can be lived with a freedom that is not canceled when we find ourselves with diverse people, diverse religious beliefs, or even the newness of oneself.

The selected writings in this book begin with the foundation of religious experience. In Thurman's spirituality, religious experience is essential for security and confidence in God. Religious experience brings the acute awareness of self and community. This awareness is not a once-and-for-all perception. Clarity about the self and community evolves as one experiences the great teacher — Life. Clarity about the meaning of religious experiences evolves as Life is lived in a disciplined way that enables spiritual discernment. Spiritual truth comes with giving oneself to the journey. Life is forever offering new revelations to meet the new realities and demands of Life itself. So religious belief can never be static. Belief must be "fluid" not only to honor a *new sense* of God's will and activity, but also to embrace God's freedom to become new.[10]

Rather than a theological system that is complete, Thurman's spirituality is more an invitation to participate faithfully in caring opportunities, questions, convictions, and challenges of Christian faith. For Thurman, however, responding to such an invitation is possible only with the assurance of God's loving presence. Religious experience, community, and the self — all three — are places where God is met and revealed. All three are places of discernment for God's dream for us. All three are places where God's assurance enables life to be lived fully, faithfully, and with joy.

Notes

1. Howard Thurman, *With Head and Heart: The Autobiography of Howard Thurman* (New York: Harcourt Brace & Company; A Harvest Book, 1979), 60.

2. Roberta Byrd Barr, interview with Howard Thurman, Seattle, Washington, January 1969.

3. Thurman, *With Head and Heart*, 73–74.

4. Ibid., 77.

5. Howard Thurman, *Mysticism and the Experience of Love* (Wallingford, PA: Pendle Hill, 1961), 3.

6. Thurman, *With Head and Heart*, 162.

7. Howard Thurman, *Deep River* and *The Negro Spiritual Speaks of Life and Death* (Richmond, IN: Friends United Press, 1975), 135. These two books were originally published as separate titles, but are now available as a single volume.

8. Howard Thurman, *Jesus and the Disinherited* (Nashville: Abingdon, 1949), 34.

9. Thurman, *With Head and Heart*, 143.

10. A comprehensive interpretation of Howard Thurman's ideas and social witness can be found in my book *Howard Thurman: The Mystic as Prophet* (Richmond, IN: Friends United Press, 1991).

Chapter 1

Religious Experience:
Encountering God

Howard Thurman believes religious experience is not only essential for living as a person of faith, but also for knowing life in its fullest possible significance. He defines religious experience as the "conscious and direct exposure of the individual to God." This experience of God may be activated by an inner awareness that bursts forth in one's consciousness, or the experience may occur because of one's contemplation of nature, art, worship, or ideas. Relationships with other persons can also activate religious experience — especially relationships characterized by love.

Thurman is a mystic. He describes mysticism as a form of religious experience where the awareness of a "conscious and direct exposure" to God is more intense. Thurman does not consider mysticism as a superior religious experience, only different. In fact, most of his writing and speaking about religious experience do not specifically refer to mysticism. Still, his mystic consciousness informs all his insights.

Through religious experience, asserts Thurman, the individual comes to know God's loving presence in a personal and private way. This knowledge provides the individual a sense of *ultimate security and confidence. Life takes on a new focus requiring a reassessment of the adequacy of one's commitment to God.*

Spiritual disciplines are essential to religious experience. These disciplines "ready" the individual for religious experience, and they are the means for understanding and enacting the insights that may follow. Throughout his writing, Thurman mentions numerous spiritual practices. In Disciplines of the Spirit, *however, he focuses on five disciplines: commitment, growth, suffering, prayer, and reconciliation. The identification of "suffering" as a discipline marks a distinction from the common tendency to treat suffering as something to be avoided. Thurman understands that there are times when suffering is the consequence of oppression, accidents, and disease. He advocates doing whatever one can, within ethical limits, to avoid such suffering. Still, suffering can also be a* choice. *Our commitment may clearly involve situations where suffering is either highly likely or assured. If, for fear of suffering, we fail to follow our commitment, then the fear of suffering has greater power over us than God. Under these circumstances, the choice of suffering can be a faithful response to the commitment that results from religious experience.*

The new focus and commitment resulting from religious experience (and for Christians, from following the example of Jesus) inspire the desire to transform not only oneself, but also the world. Religious experience is thus crucial to both personal and social transformation.

Thurman is intensely interested in the religious experience of Jesus. He believes that we best understand the witness of Jesus as a response to his personal encounters with God. Jesus models the importance of religious experience as it relates to religious commitment and the practice of spiritual disciplines. Thurman thinks of Jesus as an intimate friend whose life reveals what it means to surrender oneself to God. In following Jesus, Christians come to know spiritual authority and power for engaging life according to God's desires.

Thurman challenges the church to accept its responsibility in nurturing persons for religious experience and spiritual practice. He laments the tendency of the church to substitute creeds, doctrines, dogma, and ritual for religious experience. To be clear, Thurman believes these are resources for spiritual formation; however, they should not be considered replacements for the God-encounter that occurs in religious experience.

Religious experience and spiritual disciplines provide the foundation of every chapter of this book. By locating them in this first chapter, their significance and purpose are introduced. They are fundamental to defining, forming, and transforming both community and the self. Thurman believes that the Oneness of religious experience is the world's only hope for peace. Considering that religion has been the source of much of the world's conflict, this hope might appear misplaced. Yet the realization and power that come from encountering God eventually lead to the transformation of religion. This is the basis of Thurman's hope that the Oneness of religious experience will one day overcome the divisions among adherents of religions and within a violent world.

DEEP CALLS UNTO DEEP

Religious experience is interpreted to mean the conscious and direct exposure of the individual to God. Such an experience seems to the individual to be inclusive of all the meaning of his life — there is nothing that is not involved. There is present here what William James refers to as "acquaintance-knowledge" as contrasted with "knowledge about." It is immediate experience and yet experience that is purely immediate is not quite possible. The individual is never an isolated, independent unit. He brings to his religious experience certain structural and ideological equipment or tools. This equipment is apt to be very determinative in how he interprets the significance not only of his religious experience but also the significance of experience itself.

It is a rather curious paradox, and yet not altogether curious this idea, this fact rather, that the individual is very importantly an experiencer. All of the details of his experience, that is, the raw materials of his experience, are in some very crucial manner worked over by him, assimilated by him, and thus they become parts of what he defines as his own person, his own personality, or his own self. But the individual is never completely one with his experiences. He remains always observer and participant. This is very important to remember.

— *The Creative Encounter,* 20–21

•

There is present in religious experience an original and direct element which seems to be in, and of itself, intrinsic and supremely worthful. By this original and direct element, I do not mean some special religious organ or some unique religious element in the personality. But there is the aspect *extraordinary* in religious experience. But what?

It is in order to seek an answer to this question. The central fact in religious experience is the awareness of meeting God. The descriptive words used are varied: sometimes it is called an encounter; sometimes, a confrontation; and sometimes, a sense of Presence. What is insisted upon, however, without regard to the term used, is that in the experience defined as religious, the individual is seen as being exposed to direct knowledge of ultimate meaning, *ne plus ultra* being, in which all that the individual is, becomes clear as immediate and often distinct rev-elation. He is face to face with something which is so much more, and so much more inclusive, than all of his awareness of himself that for him, *in the moment,* there are no questions. Without asking, somehow he knows.

The mind apprehends the whole — the experience is beyond or inclusive of the discursive. It is not other than the discursive, but somehow it is inclusive of the discursive. As Bennett puts it, "It is the knowledge of the subject of all predicates." It is precisely because of this synoptic apprehension that the individ-ual in the experience seems to come into possession of what he has known as being true all along. The thing that is new is the *realization.* And this is of profound importance.

— *The Creative Encounter,* 23–24

There is in all intuition the element of revelation which may be characterized as the leaping element. This aspect of intu-ition makes it throw light on known materials; and the thing that makes it an intuition is the fact that it establishes clearly and definitely what was known peripherally, vaguely, or merely dimly sensed. The intuition says that I bring you knowledge which has been there and in you all along. Such intuition serves a very important purpose in religious experience for it is the in-tuition that finally takes on a molding and tutoring character which gives content, in terms of concept, to the body of belief which becomes the individual's religious equipment. It must be kept in mind that, how the person relates the intuition to the context of his life so that it becomes a handle by which he is able to connect himself with the living world of living events, is determined by the equipment which he brings to the experience.

— *The Creative Encounter,* 47

•

The goal of life is God! The source of life is God! That out of which life comes is that into which life goes. He out of whom life comes is He into whom life goes. God is the goal of man's life, the end of all his seeking, the meaning of all his striving. God is the guarantor of all his values, the ultimate meaning — the timeless frame of reference. That which sustains the flower of the field, the circling series of stars in the heavens, the structure of dependability in the world of nature everywhere, the stirring of the will of man to action, the dream of humanity, developed and free, for which myriad men, sometimes in solitariness in lonely places or in great throngs milling in crowded squares — all this and infinitely more in richness and variety and value is God. Men may be thrown from their courses — they may wander for a million years in desert and waste land, through sin and degradation, war and pestilence, hate and love — at last they must find their rest in Him. If there is that which at any time, anywhere in the universe, can ultimately withstand the divine urgency — then whatever it is that shows such strength is co-equal with God. Such a position to me is not only untenable, but is also a denial of the basic ethical monotheism that for me is the most satisfactory explanation of the meaning of life.

The source of life is God. The mystic applies this to human life when he says that there is in man an uncreated element; or in the Book of Job where it is written that his mark is in their foreheads. In the last analysis the mood of reverence that should characterize all men's dealings with each other finds its basis here. The demand to treat all human beings as ends in themselves, or the moral imperative that issues in respect for personality, finds its profound inspiration here. To deal with men on any other basis, to treat them as if there were not vibrant and vital in each one the very life of the very God, is the great blasphemy; it is the judgment that is leveled with such relentless severity on modern man. "Thou hast made us for thyself and our souls are restless till they find their rest in thee," says Augustine. Life is like a river.

> Deep River, my home is over Jordan —
> Deep River, I want to cross over into camp ground.
>
> *— Deep River*, 77–78

●

Here we are face to face with perhaps the most daring and revolutionary concept known to man: namely, that God is not only the creative mind and spirit at the core of the universe but that He — and mark you, I say He — is love. There are no completely satisfying ways by which this conclusion may be arrived at by mere or sheer rational reflective processes. This is the great disclosure: that there is at the heart of life a Heart. When such an insight is possessed by the human spirit and possesses the human spirit, a vast and awe-inspiring tranquility irradiates the life. This is the message of the spiritual ["Wade in the Water"]. Do not shrink from moving confidently out into choppy seas. Wade in the water, because God is troubling the water.

— Deep River, 95

Thou Hast Searched Me and Known Me
[Psalm 139:1]

In all places
　Where I have dallied in joyous abandon,
　Where I have responded to ancient desires and yielded
　　to impulses old as life, blinded like things that move
　　without sight;
　Where chores have remained chores, unfulfilled by
　　laziness of spirit and sluggishness of mind;

Where work has been stripped of joy by the ruthless
    pruning of vagrant ambition;
Where the task has been betrayed by slovenly effort;
Where the response to human need has been halfhearted
    and weak;
Where the surge of strength has spent itself in great
    concentration and I have been left a shaking reed in
    the wind;
Where hope has mounted until from its quivering height
    I have seen the glory and wonder of the new dawn
    of great awakening;
Where the quiet hush of utter surrender envelops me in
    the great silence of intimate commitment;
Thou hast known me!

When I have lost my way, and thick fog has shrouded
    from my view the familiar path and the lights of
    home;
When with deliberate intent I have turned my back on
    truth and peace;
When in the midst of the crowd I have sought refuge
    among the strangers;
When things to do have peopled my days with mounting
    anxiety and ever-deepening frustration;
When in loneliness I have sat in the thicket of despair
    too weak to move, to lift my head;
Thou has searched for and found me!

I cannot escape Thy Scrutiny!
I would not escape Thy Love!

— The Inward Journey, 140–41

•

Not only is faith a way of knowing, a form of knowledge, but it is also one of life's great teachers. At no point is this fact more clearly demonstrated than in an individual's growing knowledge of God. It is obvious that, in the last analysis, proof of the existence of God is quite impossible. A simple reason for this is the fact that, if there is that to which God may be finally reduced, then He is not ultimate. But let us not be led astray by this apparent abstraction. Faith teaches a man that God is. The human spirit has two fundamental demands that must be met relative to God. First, He must be vast, limitless, transcendent, all-comprehensive, so that there is no thing that is outside the wide reaches of His apprehension. The stars in the universe, the great galaxies of spatial groupings moving in endless rhythmic patterns in the trackless skies, as well as the tiny blade of grass by the roadside, are all within His grasp. The second demand is that He be personal and intimate. A man must have a sense of being cared for, of not being alone and stranded in the universe. All of us want the assurance of not being deserted *by* life nor deserted *in* life. Faith teaches us that God is — that He is the fact of life from which all other things take their meaning and reality. When Jesus prayed, he was conscious that, in his prayer, he met Presence, and this consciousness was far more important and significant than the answering of his prayer. It is for this reason primarily that God was for Jesus the answer to all the issues and the problems of life. When I, with all my mind and heart, truly seek God and give myself in prayer, I, too, meet His Presence, and then I know for myself that Jesus was right.

— *Deep Is the Hunger,* 145–46

Religious experience in its profoundest dimension is the finding of man by God and the finding of God by man. This is the inner witness. The moral quality is mandatory because the individual must be genuine in his preparation and in his motivation and in his response. His faith must be active and dynamic. It

was pointed out earlier that the individual enters the experience and/or the preparation for it with the smell of life heavy upon him. He has in him all his errors and blindness, his raw conscience and his scar tissues, all his loves and hates. In fact, all that he is as he lives life is with him in this experience. It is in his religious experience that he sees himself from another point of view. In a very real sense he is stripped of everything and he stands with no possible protection from the countenance of the Other. The things of which he is stripped are not thrown away. They are merely laid aside and with infinite patience they are seen for what they are. It is here that the great decision is made as to what will be kept and what will be discarded. A man may take a whole lifetime to put away a particular garment forever. The new center is found, and it is often like giving birth to a new self. It is small wonder that so much is made in the Christian religion of the necessity of rebirths. There need not be only one single rebirth, but again and again a man may be reborn until at last there is nothing that remains between him and God.
— *The Creative Encounter,* 39–40

•

Fundamental to our thinking is the concept that God is the Creator of life and the Creator of man, and this in itself would tend to indicate that, therefore, God and man initially have that in common which the creature would have in common with the Creator. The place at which this contention seems to be relevant is at the point of the concern and the interest which the individual has for sharing in and creating values. It is quite conceivable that if there are purposes in the mind of the Creator and if I may enter into fellowship and communication with the Creator, then I would as a result of that fellowship and communication be exposed to the vision of His purposes. The degree to which I respond to that vision do I participate formally and consciously in those purposes. Thus my commitment becomes one in which I put at the disposal of the larger and more creative purposes of the Creator my little life, my little thoughts, my little activities, my little devotions. In the living of my life I establish more and more levels of understanding of the Creator as I achieve in fact what I see in vision.

— *The Creative Encounter,* 44–45

SPIRITUAL DISCIPLINES

The place and significance of spiritual disciplines and exercises cannot be overemphasized. It is important, however, to understand what that significance is. There is no *necessitous* relationship between the disciplines and the awareness of God's presence. All disciplines of this character are meant to "ready" the mind, the emotions, the spirit. They are no guarantor of Presence.

This is the miracle, the heights and depths of wonder and awe. God reveals His Presence out of the mystery of Being. With all of my passionate endeavor, I cannot command that He obey. All of my prayers, my meditation, my *vast* and compelling urgency or need cannot order, woo or beg God into the revealing of His Presence. Even my need and my desperation cannot command Him. There is an overwhelming autonomy here; God does move in a mysterious way His wonders to perform. But He is so full of such wonderful and heartening surprises.

In the total religious experience we learn how to wait; we learn how to ready the mind and the spirit. It is in the waiting, brooding, lingering, tarrying timeless moments that the essence of the religious experience becomes most fruitful. It is here that I learn to listen, to swing wide the very doors of my being, to clean out the corners and the crevices of my life — so that when His Presence invades, I am free to enjoy His coming to Himself in me.

In fine, I cannot command; I work at preparing my mind, my spirit for the moment when God comes to Himself in me. When it happens, I experience His Presence. When this experience becomes an object of thought and reflection, it is then that my mind creates dogmas, creeds and doctrines. These are the creations of the mind and are therefore always *after* the fact of the religious experience. But they are always out of date. The religious experience is always current, always fresh. In it I hear His Voice in my own tongue and in accordance with the grain in my own wood. In that glorious and transcendent moment, it may easily seem to me that all there is, is God.

— *Temptations of Jesus*, 14–15

Commitment

The meaning of commitment as a discipline of the spirit must take into account that mind and spirit cannot be separated from the body in any absolute sense. It has been wisely said that the time and the place of man's life on earth is the time and the place of his body, but the meaning of his life is as significant and eternal as he wills to make it. While he is on earth, his mind and spirit are domiciled in his body, bound up in a creature who is at once a child of nature and of God. Commitment means that it is possible for a man to yield the nerve center of his consent to a purpose or cause, a movement or an ideal, which may be more important to him than whether he lives or dies. The commitment is a self-conscious act of will by which he affirms his identification with what he is committed to. The character of his commitment is determined by that to which the center or core of his consent is given.

This does not mean, necessarily, that the quality and depth of a man's commitment are of the same order as what he is committed to. There is a dynamic inherent in commitment itself which seems to be independent of what the commitment is focused on. This is an important distinction, always to be borne in mind. Here again we encounter the same basic notion discovered above: there seems to be a certain automatic element in commitment, once it is set in motion. There are a mode of procedure and a sense of priority — one might say, an etiquette and a morality — that belong automatically to this kind of experience, once it becomes operative. In other words, once the conditions are met, energy becomes available in accordance with what seems a well-established pattern of behavior. What is true for plants and animals other than man seems to be true for man. There are many complexities introduced as we observe the pattern at the level of mind, but they must not confuse the basic, elemental fact. When the conditions are met, the energy of life is made available....

Serious problems arise when the same principle operates in the conscious activities of man. There is a sense, alas, in which it is true that the wicked do prosper. When a man who has an evil heart gives the nerve center of his consent to evil enterprise, he does receive energy and strength. The most casual observation confirms this in human experience. There is a vitality in the demonic enterprise when it becomes the fundamental commitment of a life. However, the Christian view insists that ultimately the evil enterprise will not be sustained by life, for the simple reason that it is *against* life. What is against life will be destroyed by life, for what is against life is against God. Nevertheless, there is a time interval when nothing is in evidence that can distinguish the quality or integrity of an evil commitment from a good one. This is at least one of the important insights in the Master's parable of the wheat and the tares. There is a period in their growth when they cannot be distinguished or separated from each other. Ultimately the wheat bears fruit proper to itself, and the tares are only tares. But meanwhile the issue is not clear, not clear at all. Again, the Master says that God "makes his sun rise on the evil and the good, and sends rain on the

just and unjust." We seem to be in the presence of a broad and all-comprehending rhythm. There is a logic and an order in the universe in which all living things, at least, are deeply involved.
— *Disciplines of the Spirit,* 17, 18

•

In Christianity there is ever the central, inescapable demand of surrender. The assumption is that this is well within the power of the individual. If the power is lacking, every effort must be put forth to find out what the hindrance is. No exception is permissible. "If the eye is a hindrance, pluck it out...if the arm is a hindrance, cut it off." Whatever stands in the way of the complete and full surrender, we must search it out and remove it. If a bad relationship is a hindrance, one must clean it up. In other words, whatever roadblocks appear, the individual must remove them. The yielding of the very nerve center of one's consent is a private, personal act in which a human being, as sovereign, says "Yes." The ability to do this, to say "Yes," is not the result of any special talent, gift, or endowment. It is not the product of any particular status due to birth, social definition, race, or national origin. It is not a power one can exercise only if given the right by one's fellows. It is not contingent upon wealth or poverty, sickness or health, creed or absence of creed. No, the demand is direct and simple: Surrender your inner consent to God — this is your sovereign right — this is your birthright privilege. And a man can do it directly and in his own name. For this he needs no special sponsorship. He yields *his* heart to God and in so doing experiences for the first time a sense of coming home and of being at home.
— *Disciplines of the Spirit,* 19–20

The dynamics inherent in the surrender become immediately available to the life of the surrendered person. His life is given back to him at another level. Literally he loses his life and finds it. In the surrender to God in the religious experience there is no loss of being but rather an irradiation of the self that makes it alive with "Godness" and in various ways. There is awakened the desire to be Godlike. This is no vague pious wish, no moist-eyed sentimentality, but rather a robust affirmation of the whole spirit of the man. This is no casual interest in superficial goodness. It is goodness at its profoundest depth. It is this kind of goodness which must have been in the mind of Jesus when someone addressed him as Good Master and he said, "Why callest thou me good? there is none good but God." To be good as God is good becomes the overwhelming desire. This means goodness not in contrast with evil, but goodness in terms of wholeness, for lack of a better term, of integration. Or again perhaps more crucially in terms of creative synthesis. There must be about God an "altogetherness" in which all conflict is resolved and all tensions merge into a single integration.

— *The Creative Encounter*, 75–76

I had no idea of the procedure for ordination as set forth by the [Baptist] churches of Virginia. I asked for permission to prepare and read a statement of faith. It was highly irregular, I was told, but my request was granted. Then I brashly announced that I did not want the laying on of hands during the prayer of ordination. This custom was altogether too old-fashioned, I argued, with all the arrogance of youth. At this point Cousin Arthur balked. "There will be the laying on of hands or there will be no ordination."

The day came. Dr. Owen arrived before noon. We gathered in the sanctuary. After all the delegates had been duly registered, the presiding minister turned the meeting over to an officer of the council, who served as the "catechizer." I read my statement of faith, which was preceded by an announcement that this was an unusual procedure and was granted as a special favor to the host minister. Then the questions began, running the gamut of religious doctrine within the scope of Virginia Baptist orthodoxy. The hours dragged on. After more than four hours of questioning, we were all exhausted and irritable. Finally, the secretary of the council, a young pastor who was a student and not much older than myself, raised the question of evolution. The Scopes trial was being held at the time. He spoke at length before coming to his question. "What does this young man really think about the inspiration of the Holy Scriptures? What he read from that piece of paper about the word of God could be said about Bryant's *Thanatopsis.*" But he had talked so long to make his point that before I could respond, a motion was made to dismiss me, that my case might be discussed and a vote taken. It was duly seconded, but on the "question" the eldest minister said, "I would like to ask our younger brother only one question: When did God the Father and God the Son and God the Holy Spirit meet for the first time?" When I replied to the catechizer, in weariness and frustration, "I don't know, because I wasn't there," everybody laughed. Looking straight into my eyes, he answered his own question. "It was at the baptism of our Lord. I pray that They may see fit to meet in your heart." His words ended the meeting.

The ceremony of ordination was held at eight o'clock in the evening, and the moment of transcendent glory was for me the laying on of hands, which I had so strongly resisted. During the performance of this ancient and beautiful ritual "the heavens opened and the spirit descended like a dove." Ever since, when it seems that I am deserted by the Voice that called me forth, I know that if I can find my way back to that moment, the clouds will lift and the path before me will once again be clear and beckoning.   — *With Head and Heart,* 57–58

The religious experience as I have known it seems to swing wide the door, not merely into Life but into lives. I am confident that my own call to the religious vocation cannot be separated from the slowly emerging disclosure that my religious experience makes it possible for me to experience myself as a human being and thus keep a very real psychological distance between myself and the hostilities of my environment. Through the years it has driven me more and more to seek to make as a normal part of my relations with men the experiencing of them as human beings. When this happens love has essential materials with which to work. And contrary to the general religious teaching, men would not need to stretch themselves out of shape in order to love. On the contrary, a man comes into possession of himself more completely when he is *free* to love another. — *The Luminous Darkness,* 111

Growth

Growth means development in the life of an organism. It means change manifest in structure. In highly developed organisms such as man, growth means change in structure and quality of character. Generally it does not mean random development — an irresponsive or irresponsible change. Perhaps there is no such thing as random development. The term suggests lack of understanding of the process at work in an organism, a lack which causes the development to seem out of line or out of character. This is because inherent in the concept of growth is a certain ordered quality, an orderliness of plan. The lines along which the growth of any particular form of life takes place are fundamental to that form itself.

— *Disciplines of the Spirit,* 38

•

If the response of the parents or others [to a child's commands for attention] continues to be available on demand, the conscious or unconscious intent being to keep the time interval at zero between wish and fulfillment, the baby begins to get a false conditioning about the world and his place in it. For if he grows up expecting and regarding as his due that to wish is to have his wish fulfilled, then he is apt to become a permanent cripple. There are many adults who for various reasons have escaped this essential discipline of their spirit. True, in terms of physical and intellectual development they have continued to grow. Their bodies and minds have moved through all the intervening stages to maturity, but they have remained essentially babies in what they expect of life. They have a distorted conception of their own lives in particular and of life in general....

The effort to shorten the interval is natural to growth; to know when waiting is essential to the process and to the life of the individual is to be disciplined in one's spirit. To learn how to wait is to discover one of the precious ingredients in the spiritual unfolding of life, the foundation for the human attribute of patience. This is not to imply that patience is always a virtue, always desirable. Sometimes it is merely an escape into inaction because of fear or cowardice or laziness. Sometimes it may be sheer confusion in the presence of a demand that overwhelms and engulfs. What seems to be patience may be a state of inertia, the result of unyielding weariness or exhaustion. As such it is sterile and lifeless.   —*Disciplines of the Spirit*, 41, 42

•

Growth also means the experience of crisis. This is a form of tension. In the growing child tension has the same basic elements that are present in the dynamics of crisis wherever found. It is created by two forces making contradictory demands simultaneously. On the one hand there is the push toward the new, the unexplored, the unknown and untried. This is the essential pull of all adventure. It causes the child to "get into trouble" with his environment because he is always upsetting something that is fixed in its place. It makes him try to open all closed doors, pull out bureau drawers, get the feel of fire, experiment with electric outlets — the list is as long as it is hazardous. The restlessness seems to be innate and is not at first geared to specific desire or intent....

But this is not the whole story of the anatomy of crisis. There is another impulse at work, as authentic as that just noted. It is the inner urge to pull back, to withdraw, to stay put, to *hold*, as it were — an unadmitted, perhaps unconscious intent to conserve, consolidate, hold the line against change and all its sundry implications. The child knows this as part of his experience of growth. Often he shrinks from the new, the untried. It seems quite natural to be frightened of the strange or the unfamiliar. The tendency seems more pronounced during certain periods of childhood than in others. At such times, to become identified with the unfamiliar is to be threatened with isolation from the group. To get out of step in dress or language is to be exposed to marked penalties....

Thus this principle of growth is involved even in the resolution of tension. The tension cannot stand indefinitely. It has to be resolved in one way or another. The resolution is in terms of holding back or letting go, of staying put or moving ahead. In fact, it is in terms of change, and this is true even if the decision appears to fall on the side of no movement or no change. For, once the crisis is made plain and the decision taken against change, a different basis for continuing has emerged. The situation is never as it was before the issue was faced or forced.
— *Disciplines of the Spirit,* 48–51, 53

•

Growth always involves the risk of failure to fulfill what is implicit in a particular life, its potential....

The possibility of error is essential to any understanding of the significance of mistakes. The error potential inherent in human life, geared as it is to the finitude of man's existence, is at least one of the major marks of distinction between man and other animals or forms of life. As a creature, he is bound in his body by the tendency inherent in the form of life he represents. His body grows as other bodies grow. The life in him fulfills itself, or works toward that fulfillment, in what we have seen as a tendency to goal-seeking inherent in life even in its simplest forms.... Man is more than a creature, he has a mark of the image of God in him; he is a creator of worlds, a dreamer of dreams, and a fashioner of kingdoms. As such, he is involved in a context of relationships which he shares with his fellows, and what he does at any particular moment or in any given circumstance involves others as well as himself. Thus his responsibility for his actions, his choices, is in effect not confined to himself. This fact alone has much to do with the constant threat of error. Though a man make a private or personal choice, its bearing on the lives of others is ever present....

Never to be forgotten is the fact that the real possibility of failure, deriving from the constant threat of error, is one of the real challenges of growth. To guard against this and be prepared to deal with it when it occurs is an authentic discipline of the spirit. To be victimized by error and at the same time keep on making choices with integrity is to grow in grace. And for the religious man, it is to grow not only in grace but also in the knowledge and experience of God.

— Disciplines of the Spirit, 55, 57, 58

Suffering

Suffering is always pain in some form. A thing that is not capable of feeling pain cannot suffer. A simple working definition is that suffering is physical pain or its equivalent, with reference to which the individual may be inspired to protect himself, so that despite its effects he may carry on the functioning of his life.

— Disciplines of the Spirit, 66

In the first place, when a man is driven by suffering to make the most fundamental inquiries concerning the meaning of life, he has to assess and re-assess his total experience. It may be that he has never seriously thought about the meaning behind the energy of a simple act. He has never thought seriously about God. He has taken his life and all life for granted. Now under the assault of pain he is led to wonder about the mystery of life. Why do men suffer? he asks himself. He sorts out the answers available to him, some of which we have touched upon. He may conclude, perhaps, that suffering is given; it is a part of the life contract that every living thing signs at the entrance. Therefore it must belong in and to life. It is no invasion from the outside. It is no strange phenomenon wandering at random among the children of men. And if it belongs, then it has to be accepted as a part of one's acceptance of life. To reject it is to reject life. This is the first thing that he pins down in his assessment.

If suffering belongs, then does it go along for the ride, or must it carry its end of the stick? Does it have a function? What would life be like if there were no suffering, no pain? The startling discovery is made that if there were no suffering there would be no freedom. Men could make no mistakes, consciously or unconsciously. The race could make no mistakes. There would be no error. There would be no possibility of choice at any point, or in any sense whatsoever. It is irrelevant to suggest that there might be a more satisfactory way to guarantee this than to make human misery in some sense mandatory. Freedom therefore cannot be separated from suffering. This, then, may be one of the ways in which suffering pays for its ride. . . .

Why do men suffer? They suffer as a part of the experience of freedom. They suffer as a part of the growth of life itself. They suffer as a part of life. This leaves many questions unanswered:

the pain of the innocent, the frustration of wasting illness of one kind or another. But at last we have a clue in the notion that without suffering there is no freedom for man, and that through it every man is faced with the necessity of experiencing in his being — not merely in his physical body — the meaning of death.   — *Disciplines of the Spirit*, 80–81

•

What hostility may do is to serve as a guide through the wilderness of our suffering until we are brought to the door of the temple. When we face God with our hostility, a kind of ultimate suction takes place which empties us completely. This is achieved in our confession to Him about how we feel toward Him, toward life and perhaps toward ourselves about our suffering. Out of our struggle we may be given insight into the suffering itself; we may be given quiet assurance, or we may relax our intent into His Purpose, or we may turn it over to Him in quiet obedience. But this must be truly done.

I sat by a lady on the train one day who talked incessantly about nothing in particular. Suddenly she turned to me and asked, "Do you believe in prayer?" I replied very slowly, "Yes." "So do I," she said, quick as a flash. Continuing, she said, "Before I left home today, I took all of my troubles" — here she digressed for twenty minutes to fill in details — "made them into a neat bundle and handed them over to God; but before He could get the bundle unwrapped to take a look, I snatched them back again." It is this mood that must be guarded against in our suffering in relation to religious experience. It is particularly relevant because hostility tends to keep up the illusion of self-importance and pride. There are many people who would feel cheated if suddenly they were deprived of the ego definition that their suffering gives them.

— *The Creative Encounter*, 52–53

Prayer

In the first place prayer, in the sense in which I am using it, means the *method* by which the individual makes his way to the temple of quiet within his own spirit and the *activity* of his spirit within its walls. Prayer is not only the participation in communication with God in the encounter of religious experience, but it is also the "readying" of the spirit for such communication. It is the total process of quieting down and to that extent must not be separated from meditation. Perhaps, as important as prayer itself, is the "readying" of the spirit for the experience.

In such "readying" a quiet place is very important if not altogether mandatory. In the noise of our times such a place may be impossible to find. One of the great services that the Christian church can render to the community is to provide spells and spaces of quiet for the world-weary men and women whose needs are so desperate. . . .

When one has been thus prepared, a strange thing happens. It is very difficult to put into words. The initiative slips out of one's hands and into the hands of God, the other Principal in the religious experience. The self moves toward God. Such movement seems to have the quality of innate and fundamental stirring. The self does not see itself as being violated, though it may be challenged, stimulated, inspired, conditioned, but all of this takes place in a frame of reference that is completely permissive. There is another movement which is at once merged with the movement of the self. God touches the spirit and the will and a wholly new character in terms of dimension enters the experience. In this sense prayer may be regarded as an open-end experience.

Fundamental to the total fact of prayer in the Christian religion is the persuasive affirmation that the God of religious experience is a seeking and a beseeching God. "O Jerusalem, Jerusalem, . . . how often would I have gathered thy children together, even as a hen gathereth her chickens under her wings, and ye would not." The great parables of "The Lost Sheep," "The Lost Coin," and "The Prodigal Son" carry the same idea. The discovery of such a fact in one's experience in life is first met in the religious experience itself.

— The Creative Encounter, 34–35, 37–38

•

The experience of communion [with God through prayer] may elicit an expression of concern for someone whose need is great or for whom one has compelling love. Such a person may be ill, or in trouble, or in deep quandary before the exacting demands of a fateful decision. To bring him and his need clearly to mind, or into complete focus, and expose him tenderly to the scrutiny and love of God through our own thought is to pray for him. At such a moment questions as to the efficacy of intercessory prayer becomes merely academic. I share my concern with God and leave the rest to Him. Does such a sharing do any good? Does it make a difference? The conviction of the praying person is that it does some good, that it does make a difference. Can you prove it, he may be asked. In what does proof of such a thing consist? The question of the effectiveness of intercessory prayer does not belong in the experience of the man who prays for his friend — it is his care that is poured out when he is most conscious of being cared for himself. When the hunger for God becomes articulate in a man so that it is one with his initial experience of God, it is the most natural thing in the world to share whatever his concerns may be. A man prays for loved ones because he has to, not merely because his prayer may accomplish something beyond this.

There is no attempt here to deal with the problems and issues that center in a discussion of what is called intercessory prayer. With reference to these I permit myself one comment only. The man who shares his concern for others with God in prayer does two things at the same time. He exposes the need of the other person to his total life and resources, making it possible for new insights of helpfulness and creativity to emerge in him. In other words he sees more clearly how to relate himself to the other person's need. In the second place, he may quicken the spirit of his friend to a sudden upsurging of the hunger for God, with the result that he is in the way of help from the vast creative energies of God. How this is done we may speculate but never explain. That it happens again and again in the religious experience of the race is a part of the data of the prayer experience itself....

The communion may be an overflowing of thanksgiving. Here I do not mean an order of thanks for services rendered or for good received. Here is no perfunctory grace before meals, when a person chooses to mumble gratitude either out of habit, or superstition, or because of spiritual breeding of a high order. No, I do not mean this sort of thing, but rather the overflowing of the heart as an act of grace toward God. The overflow is not merely because of what has taken place in life or in the world or because of all the manifestations of benevolence that have covered a life. Something far more profound is at work. It is akin to adoration; it is the sheer joy in thanksgiving that God is God and the soul is privileged and blessed with the overwhelming consciousness of this. It is the kind of thanksgiving that sings itself to the Lord because He is God. This praiseful thanksgiving overshadows any bill of particulars, even though many particular things crowd into mind. We can get some notion of what is meant here when, under some circumstances, we encounter a person who, for what seems to be a swirling temporary moment, enjoys *us* — not what we say or what we are doing or what we represent, but who reaches into the core of our being and touches us purely. How such moments must rejoice the heart of God! I agree most heartily with Rufus Jones

when he says that prayer at its best is when the soul enjoys God
and prays out of sheer love of Him.

— *Disciplines of the Spirit,* 100–101, 102

•

We must find sources of strength and renewal for our own spirits, lest we perish. There is a wide spread recognition of the need
for refreshment of the mind and the heart. It is very much in
order to make certain concrete suggestions in this regard. First,
we must learn to be quiet, to settle down in one spot for a spell.
Sometime during each day, everything should stop and the art
of being still must be practiced. For some temperaments, it will
not be easy because the entire nervous system and body have
been geared over the years to activity, to overt and tense functions. Nevertheless, the art of being still must be practiced until
development and habit are sure. If possible, find a comfortable
chair or quiet spot where one may engage in nothing. There
is no reading of a book or a paper, no thinking of the next
course of action, no rejecting of remote or immediate mistakes
of the past, no talk. One is engaged in doing nothing at all except being still. At first one may get drowsy and actually go
to sleep. The time will come, however, when one may be quiet
for a spell without drowsiness, but with a quality of creative
lassitude that makes for renewal of mind and body. Such periods may be snatched from the greedy demands of one's day's
work; they may be islanded in a sea of other human beings;
they may come only at the end of the day, or in the quiet hush
of the early morning. We must, each one of us, find his own
time and develop his own peculiar art of being quiet. We must
lose our fear of rest. There are some of us who keep up our
morale (morale has been defined as a belief in one's cause) by
being always busy. We have made a fetish of fevered action.
We build up our own sense of security by trying to provide a

relentless, advantageous contrast between ourselves and others by the fevered, intense activities in which we are engaged. Actually, such people are afraid of quiet. Again, most activities become a substitute for the hard-won core of purpose and direction. The time will come when all activities are depressing and heavy, and the dreaded question, "What's the use?" will have to be faced and dealt with. The first step in the discovery of sources of strength and renewal is to develop the art of being still, physical and mental cessation from churning. This is not all, but it is the point at which we begin.

—*Deep Is the Hunger,* 175–76

Some Centering Moment

We wait in the quietness for some centering moment that will redefine, reshape, and refocus our lives. It does seem to be a luxury to be able to give thought and time to the ups and downs of one's private journey while the world around is so sick and weary and desperate. But, our Father, we cannot get through to the great anxieties that surround us until, somehow, a path is found through the little anxieties that beset us. Dost Thou understand what it is like to be caught between the agony of one's own private needs and to be tempest-tossed by needs that overwhelm and stagger the mind and paralyze the heart? Dost Thou understand this, our Father?

For the long loneliness, the deep and searching joy and satisfaction, the boundless vision — all these things that give to Thee so strong a place in a world so weak — we thank Thee, Father. For whatever little grace Thou wilt give to Thy children even as they wait in confidence and stillness in Thy presence, we praise Thee. O love of God, love of God, where would we be without Thee? Where?   —*The Centering Moment,* 85

We Don't Know How

We find it very difficult, our Father, to bring to a point of focus all of the fragmentation and divisiveness of our lives. We ask Thee to draw upon Thy long experience with Thy children, and out of this special wisdom and understanding, to interpret the words which we say to Thee in our prayer. We are overwhelmed by our great inability somehow to manage the imperfections of life, the imperfections of our own private lives, the clear insight which suddenly becomes dim and often disappears at the moment when we are sure that we could act upon it; the good deed which we express and which, as it leaves us, wings on its way to fulfill itself in another's life, in another's need. And as we watch, we are horrified at the way in which something goes wrong and the good deed is not a good deed in the way in which it works, and we are thrown back upon ourselves. We don't know how to manage the imperfections of our lives, the imperfections of so many expressions of our lives.

We have brooded over nature. We have understood here and there some of its inner mandates, and we have been able to translate these mandates into expressions of machinery and objects, and we have learned how to operate these machines and to make these objects, created out of our insights, expressions of our intent. We have made these things into servants to obey our minds and our wills and then, suddenly, we are faced with radical and quick and devastating breakdown! Something goes wrong, we do not know what, and there is mindless violence and destruction. We don't know how to manage the imperfections of our lives.

Now we wait for the fateful moment when once again we ourselves as a nation will begin learning, with more finesse and accuracy, to kill, to destroy. And we feel, some of us, that the only way to survive is to do this, and some of us are sure that this is but to hasten the end of the age.

How to manage the imperfections of our minds and our spirits, our thoughts, even our intent? O God, we don't know how. We don't know how. We don't know how. Take all the outcry of our anguish, all the sin and brokenness of our faltering selves and hold them with such sureness that we learn from Thee.

— *The Centering Moment*, 103

Thou Dost Not Become Weary

It is our faith and our confidence, our Father, that Thou dost not become weary, because always before Thee we present the same sorry spectacle. It is our trust that Thou dost not get tired of us but that always Thou dost remain constant, even as we do not; that Thou dost remain true even when we take refuge in falsehood and error; that Thou dost remain kind and gracious when our hearts are hard and callous; that Thy scrutiny and Thy judgment hold despite all of our whimpering, self-pity, and shame. It is so good to have this kind of assurance and to know, as we move into the days and the hours that are still left to us, that we are not alone but that we are comforted and straightened by Thy brooding presence.

We would ask forgiveness of our sins, but of so much that is sinful in us we have no awareness. We would seek to offer to Thee the salutation of our spirits and our minds were we able to tear ourselves away from preoccupation with our own concerns, our own anxieties, our own little lives. We would give to Thee the "nerve center" of our consent if for one swirling moment we could trust Thee to do with us what our lives can stand.

O God, our Father, take the chaos and confusion and disorder of our minds and spirits and hold them so completely in Thy grasp that the impure thing will become pure, the crooked thing will become straight, and the crass and hard thing will

be gentled by Thy spirit. Oh, that we may have the strength to
see and the vision to comprehend what in us is needful for Thy
peace.   — *The Centering Moment*, 112

Reconciliation

[*More selections regarding this discipline are presented in the
section "Nonviolence and Reconciling Community," p. 121
below.*]

The discipline of reconciliation for the religious man cannot
be separated from the discipline of religious experience. In religious experience a man has a sense of being touched at his
inmost center, at his very core, and this awareness sets in motion the process that makes for his integration, his wholeness.
It is as if he saw into himself, beyond all his fragmentation,
conflicts, and divisiveness, and recognized his true self. The
experience of the prodigal son is underscored in the religious
experience of the race — when he came to himself, he came to
his father's house and dwelling place. The experience of God
reconciles all the warring parts that are ultimately involved in
the life of every man as against whatever keeps alive the conflict, and its work is healing and ever redemptive. Therefore
there is laid upon the individual the need to keep the way open
so that he and his Father may have free and easy access to
each other.

Such is the ethical imperative of religious experience. This
is not to suggest that religion is the only basis of the ethical
imperative, but to state clearly that such an imperative is central
to the religious experience. "So if you are offering your gift at
the altar, and there remember that your brother has something
against you, leave your gift there before the altar and go; first be
reconciled to your brother, and then come and offer your gift"
(Matt. 5:23–24).   — *Disciplines of the Spirit*, 121–22

THE EXEMPLARY JESUS

When the individual's life comes under the influence of the God of his religious exposure, then the stage may be set for a soul-shaking conflict of loyalty. At last he must decide without regard to the bearing of the decision on his loyalty to the group. This decision calls for something much more coherent and intelligible than a mere feeling that this is what God demands of him. It is here that the concept of incarnation in the Christian faith takes on a practical significance. How does the individual know that his obedience is to God? Can he trust his interpretation of his finding, his residue of religious experience? The way is open now for some form of authority. The Christian finds the clue to his answer, yet even more than this, he finds the answers themselves, in the life and teachings of Jesus. Jesus becomes for such a view the *for instance* of the mind of God in reach of the tools of the individual. He *may* say, "I do not know what God requires. I'm not sure I can depend upon what seems to me the definite or definitive will of God. I am a creature of error, but I can know Jesus through the gospel and I share in the claim which is made for him and that he is the word made flesh. He is in reach, and he can give me a tested series of formulae for the guidance of my own life because of the shared commitment which is ours. The study of his life thus becomes a necessity of my commitment."

Any personal behavior, then, that is out of harmony with his life and teaching becomes exposed to the swift judgment of what seems to me now to be his spirit. Slowly his mind becomes my mind, and then the amazing discovery that the mind that is more and more in me is the mind that was more and more in him. The mind that was in him becomes more and more clearly to me to be the mind that is God. All of this may be achieved without any necessity whatsoever of making a God out of Jesus.
— *The Creative Encounter*, 82–83

•

Few of the spirituals have to do with the nativity of Christ. This has given rise to many speculations. James Weldon Johnson was of the opinion that the fact that Christmas Day was a day of special license having no religious significance to slaves, is largely responsible. My own opinion somewhat concurs. It should be added that, in the teaching of the Bible stories concerning the birth of Jesus, very little appeal was made to the imagination of the slave because it was not felt wise to teach him the significance of this event to the poor and the captive. It was dangerous to let the slave understand that the life and teachings of Jesus meant freedom for the captive and release for those held in economic, social, and political bondage. Even now these implications are not lifted to the fore in much of the contemporary emphasis upon Jesus. It is of first-rate significance to me that Jesus was born of poor parentage; so poor indeed was he that his parents could not offer even a lamb for the sacrifice but had to use doves instead. Unlike the Apostle Paul, he was not a Roman citizen. If a Roman soldier kicked Jesus into a Palestinian ditch he could not appeal to Caesar; it was just another Jew in the ditch. What limitless release would have been available to the slave if the introduction to Jesus had been on the basis of his role as the hope of the disinherited and the captive. In the teaching of the Christian religion to the slave this aspect of the career of Jesus was carefully overlooked, and continues to be even now. Much is said about what the Christian attitude toward the poor should be; but I have yet to hear a sermon on the meaning of the religion of Jesus to the disinherited, to the poor.   — *Deep River*, 21–22

Jesus of Nazareth had what seems to me to have been a fundamental and searching — almost devastating — experience of God. This experience was so fontal and so fundamental to the very grounds of his being that he had to deal with the

implications of this experience whenever he raised any question
about the meaning and function of his own life.

— *Temptations of Jesus*, 22

Not by Bread Alone

The spirit swept upon him
Like some winged creature from above!
Light was all around:
    Every leaf shimmered and danced,
    A swirling dervish in a timeless trance.
The sky was lost in light.
He saw and felt the light.

From all around, here, there, everywhere
The Voice whispered in tones that sang:
    "Thou art my son; this day I claim you as my
    own..."
Wrapped in the echo of the sound
He took the way beyond the city gates,
Beyond the crooked path
Where the rocks began!
He walked until wilderness, rocky ledge and quiet
Were all around. He found a resting place to wait.
When the burning cooled and his mind would ease,
    Then he would know.

Time passed making no sound and there was none to
    count the hour.

Into his mind one question came:
    What is man's life?
    Is it for bread he strives
    That dreams might last?
There is a way to hold the gate
'Gainst hunger as a common fate:

Make bread the all-absorbing aim,
And give to it a prior claim.
There would be space for inner things
For the heavy fruit of prophet's dream.
It seemed so clear what he must do.
Lost in the labyrinth of Fancy's ways,
He had not reckoned with the Voice:
    "No, not by bread alone."
It leaped into his mind like a thing possessed!
    "No, not by bread alone."
The hills picked up the words and gave them sound;
Tramped the rhythm on wind and cloud, in sky and air,
All around, everywhere:
    "No, not by bread alone.
    Man does not live by bread alone.
Out of the mouth of God
All good things come:
Truth and beauty; goodness, love —
    No, not by bread alone."

—*The Inward Journey*, 54–55

Jesus Prays

To Jesus, God breathed through all that is. The sparrow overcome by sudden death in its evening flight; the lily blossoming on the rocky hillside; the grass of the field and the garden path; the clouds light and burdenless or weighted down with unshed water; the madman in chains or wandering among the barren rocks in the wastelands; the little baby in his mother's arms; the strutting arrogance of the Roman Legion; the brazen queries of the craven tax collector; the children at play or the old men quibbling in the market place; the august Sanhedrin fighting for its life amidst the impudences of Empire; the futile whisper of those who had forgotten Jerusalem; the fear-voiced utterance of the prophets who remembered — to Jesus, God breathed through all that is. To Jesus, God was Creator of life and the living substance; the Living Stream upon which all things moved; the Mind containing time, space, and all their multitudinous offsprings. And beyond all these God was Friend and Father.

The time most precious for him was at close of day. This was the time for the long breath, when all the fragments left by the commonplace, when all the little hurts and the big aches could be absorbed, and the mind could be freed of the immediate demand, when voices that had been quieted by the long day's work could once more be heard, when there could be the deep sharing of the innermost secrets and the laying bare of the heart and mind. Yes, the time most precious for him was at close of day.

But there were other times he treasured, "A great while before day," says the Book. The night had been long and wearisome because the day had been full of nibbling annoyances; the high resolve of some winged moment had frenzied, panicked, no longer sure, no longer free, and then had vanished as if it had never been. There was need, the utter urgency, for some fresh assurance, the healing touch of a healing wing. "A great while before day" he found his way to the quiet place in the hills. And prayed.   — *The Inward Journey*, 30

The Triumphant Entry

Searching indeed must have been the thoughts moving through the mind of the Master as he jogged along on the back of the donkey on that fateful day which marks in the Christian calendar the Triumphant Entry. The experience must have been as strange and out of character for him as it was for the faithful animal on whose back he rode.

For more than two years, Jesus had been engaged in a public ministry. Once when there were those who wanted to make him a king, he had refused. "My kingdom is not of this world." He had walked the countryside with his band of disciples, preaching, teaching, healing, and spreading a quality of radiance that could come only from one whose overwhelming enthusiasm was for God and His Kingdom. He had kept many lonely trysts in the late watches of the night, trueing his spirit and his whole life by the will of his Father. So close had he worked with God that the line of demarcation between his will and God's Will would fade and reappear, fade and reappear. Step by resolute step, he had come to the great city. Deep within his spirit there may have been a sense of foreboding, or the heightened quality of exhilaration that comes from knowing that there is no road back.

He had learned much. So sensitive had grown his spirit and the living quality of his being that he seemed more and more to stand inside of life, looking out upon it as a man who gazes from a window in a room out into the yard and beyond to the distant hills. He could feel the sparrowness of the sparrow, the leprosy of the leper, the blindness of the blind, the crippleness of the cripple, and the frenzy of the mad. He had become joy, sorrow, hope, anguish, to the joyful, the sorrowful, the hopeful, the anguished. Could he feel his way into the mind and the mood of those who cast the palms and the flowers in his path? Was he in the cry of those who exclaimed their wild and unrestrained Hosannas? Did he mingle with the emotions that lay beneath the exultations ready to explode in the outburst of the mob screaming, "Crucify him! Crucify him!" I wonder what was at work in the mind of Jesus of Nazareth as he jogged along on the back of the faithful donkey.

Perhaps his mind was far away to the scenes of his childhood, feeling the sawdust between his toes, in his father's shop.

He may have been remembering the high holy days in the synagogue, with his whole body quickened by the echo of the ram's horn as it sounded. Or perhaps he was thinking of his mother, how deeply he loved her and how he wished that there had not been laid upon him the Great Necessity which sent him out on the open road to proclaim the Truth, leaving her side forever. It may be that he lived all over again that high moment on the Sabbath when he was handed the scroll and he unrolled it to the great passage from the prophet Isaiah, "The spirit of the Lord is upon me, for he has anointed me to preach the gospel to the poor, to open the eyes of the blind, to unstop the ears of the deaf, to announce the acceptable year of the Lord." I wonder what was moving through the mind of the Master as he jogged along on the back of the faithful donkey.

— The Inward Journey, 31–32

It was the celebration of the Passover, the common meal of surging remembrance. The Master and his twelve disciples were gathered around the common board. Many and varied were the thoughts that streamed in endless procession through their minds. During the last few days, a strange and ominous quality had entered into the warm intimacy of the fellowship. The smell of death was in the air. There were many things that had been left unsaid through all the previous days, but now they clamored for utterance. But there were no words made ready. As it turned out, this was the last real calm before the precipitous days ahead, ending in the lacerating moment of the crucifixion. The last common meal. In the light of the events that followed it, every single detail of the meal was highlighted with a rare and awful radiance. Every accent in retrospect told its own sure tale. There was something living once, which, if it could be recaptured, would bring again into the midst the spirit of him whose magic had led captive their spirits, and once more they would know the comfort of his presence winging near. The experience is a part of the human story. Suppose you and a friend had dinner together one evening in your home. A few days after, the word came to you that the friend was dead. You would crawl inch by inch over all the events of your last meal together: The fact that you had inadvertently given to him the chipped cup. You did not discover it until, in the candlelight, the chipped spot was revealed as he lifted it to his lips to drink. Given the fact of his passing, you read back into all the common talk of the evening many things that were not present at the time, but now are clear. Gently you put away the chipped cup. It can no longer be the common thing it was before. Perhaps in certain rare moments, when you wish particularly to have the memory of your friend very living, very present, very real, the cup is used again. It is symbolic of a whole lifetime of knowledge and sharing, which you and your friend had known. The cup becomes the reminder that you have shared deeply the spirit of your friend, and that is yours forever. Death could not touch it — he could never die. And so it would be all the way to the end. The communion service, the celebration of the last supper, stripped bare of all that devotion has done in beautiful liturgy or somber dogma, means that, when spirit invades spirit, the eternal in one man mingles with the eternal in another, transcending time, space, and all the artificial barriers by which one man is marked off, separated from his fellows. To those who have learned the mind and the teaching, the courage and the wisdom of the simple Master of Galilee, the sharing together of the common meal in the holy place is to usher into their midst spirit of his spirit and mind of his mind. "Yes," he says to all, whatever may be their faith, creed, doctrine or persuasion, "when in your fellowship you eat your common meal, remember me."   — *Deep Is the Hunger,* 161–62

•

The dilemma in the Garden is the facing of the same central problem, the same central temptation that did not ever quite desert the Master. He must fulfill the Word in him. And the Word was this: All of the children of men are children of God. The Word was the living embodiment of a way of living together that would confirm, in the stuff of life, the deep searching insistent intent of God, his Father. The dream did not stop there. How could this be done?

There is a way by which this dream, this intent, can become not merely literal truth but literal fact. In Jesus, the Kingdom was literal Truth, and the step from literal Truth to literal Fact involved implementation. To implement it men must ready themselves with moods, attitudes, feeling tones, desires, all summarized by the word Love.

But men can't do this by themselves, the dream continues. Because the dream is a part of the very intent of God, the resources of God are available on behalf of the translation of the dream from literal Truth to literal Fact. Over and over again Jesus said, "O men, how little you trust Him."

As this dream began to work, in all of its manifestations, it created tensions and pressures in the midst of a society that had not made up its mind. It is important for me to remember as I reflect upon this (and this may not be right, but it seems to me to be right) that there wasn't anything personal in this. The people who felt themselves threatened by this insistence on the part of the Master did not regard it as something that was personal and private, something that was focused or aimed at them in particular, but Jesus symbolized that which challenged and threatened the established structure. And the structure fought back, not merely because it did not like Jesus. That was not the point. The structure fought back because the structure did not want to be upset....

It is not merely that at his age, he [Jesus] didn't want to die.
That's perfectly natural, isn't it? There is nothing unusual about
that. But to die with such a sense of "my work not done." And
if I can convince myself that no one else can do the work, then
death is a terror. This is the subtlety of the spiritual paradox
that gripped his soul: The deeper the sense of commitment, the
deeper the sense of full-orbed destiny that rode through all the
reaches of his mind; the deeper his concentration, the more crucial his life seemed to be for the fulfillment of the Kingdom of
God....

I think that here Jesus is dealing with the most difficult thing
in religious commitment: To be able to give up the initiative
over your own life; to yield at the core of one's self, the nerve
center of one's consent to God; and to trust the act itself.

We do not know His mind. We cannot fathom the mystery
of God. We cannot even understand the meaning of our own
little lives, but the fierce hold that we have on our lives, again
and again, is the most real thing that we have. To relax that
and to trust God — not to run His world, not to people His
Universe, not to hold things in some kind of all-encompassing
grasp; no, but to trust God just with you, with me, to say, "It's
all right; my times are in Thy Hands" — is the most difficult
dimension of the spiritual life. It was the experience of the Master, I think after trying and doing it here and there a little, that
when he finally made the supreme and transcendent discovery
that when a man is sure of God in that way, he can stand anything that life can do to him, and even death becomes a little
thing.

When I contemplate his life and see all the little anxieties and
misgivings that I have, I am astounded, confounded by what he
did. I search the depths of my own soul to see if I may find some
kind of clue from him that will help me do the same thing, and
be answered. It may not matter whether any prayer any time
was ever answered. If I am not answered, then all the answered

prayers in the world are but confusing and confounding and distorting.   — *Temptations of Jesus*, 64–65, 66–67, 67–68

•

"My God! My God! Why hast Thou forsaken me!" According to the Gospel of Mark, these are the final words uttered by Jesus before his death. They reveal at once one of the most amazing utterances in the entire literature of religion. Here is one who was convinced that he had followed the will and the leadings of God through all the shifting scenes of his life at a most crucial moment in the development of his own people. He had experimented effectively and conclusively with love and understanding as a way of life; he had spent long hours in prayer and meditation; he had given himself with increasing intensity to a full-orbed understanding of the mind of God, whom he interpreted as Father. The logic of his life had led him to the fateful agony of the cross. He was there keeping his tryst with his Father — but where was his Father? The implication of the cry, which Jesus quotes from one of the Psalms, is that he was surer of God than God was of him. It means also that, in his moment of complete exhaustion, Jesus was making one of the great elemental discoveries about the nature of existence; namely, that often the point at which man becomes most keenly aware of the reality of God is on the lonely height, when he is stripped to the literal substance of himself, with nothing between his soul and an ultimate agony. At such a moment, God is seen as the only reality, and oneness with Him as the only fulfillment. The secondary meaning of this discovery is that the end of life and the meaning of life cannot be summarized in terms of happiness, joy, or even satisfaction. Again and again, we must discover that life may say "No" to our most cherished desires, our high hopes, our great yearning. And we must learn to live with life's "No." This is not only to discover the peace that passeth understanding, which may come when the pain of life is not relieved, but also to know for oneself that God is closest to us when, in our agony and frustration, he seems to be farthest away.

— Deep Is the Hunger, 163–64

The Light of His Spirit

In many ways beyond all calculation and reflection, our lives have been deeply touched and influenced by the character, the teaching, and spirit of Jesus of Nazareth. He moves in and out upon the horizon of our days like some fleeting ghost. At times, when we are least aware and least prepared, some startling clear thrust of his mind is our portion — the normal tempo of our ways is turned back upon itself and we are reminded of what we are, and of what life is. Often the judgment of such moments is swift and silencing: sometimes his insight kindles a wistful longing in the heart, softened by the muted cadence of unfulfilled dreams and unrealized hopes. Sometimes his words stir to life long forgotten resolutions, call to mind an earlier time when our feet were set in a good path and our plan was for holy endeavor. Like a great wind they move, fanning into flame the burning spirit of the living God, and our leaden spirits are given wings that sweep beyond all vistas and beyond all horizons.

There is no way to balance the debt we owe to the spirit which he let loose in the world. It is upon this that we meditate now in the gathering quietness. Each of us, in his own way, finds the stairs leading to the Holy Place. We gather in our hands the fragments of our lives, searching eagerly for some creative synthesis, some wholeness, some all-encompassing unity, capable of stilling the tempests within us and quieting all the inner turbulence of our fears. We seek to walk in our own path which opens up before us, made clear by the light of his spirit and the radiance which it casts all around us. We join him in the almighty trust that God is our Father and we are His children living under the shadow of His Spirit.

Accept the offering of our lives, O God; we do not know quite what to do with them. We place them before Thee as they are, encumbered and fragmented, with no hints, no suggestions, no attempts to order the working of Thy Spirit upon us. Accept our lives, our Father — work them over. Correct them. Purify them. Hold them in Thy focus lest we perish and the spirit within us dies. Amen.   — *The Inward Journey,* 126–27

THE CHURCH'S CHALLENGE

It is in order now at last to raise the question: Is the witness of the church in our society the unfolding of such an idea as we see manifested in the religious experience and the life of Jesus? Whatever may be the delimiting character of the historical development of the church, the simple fact remains that at the present moment in our society, as an institution, the church is divisive and discriminating, even within its fellowship. It is divided into dozens of splinters. This would indicate that it is essentially sectarian in character. As an institution there is no such thing as the church. There has to be some kind of church....

The concept of denominationalism seems to me to be in itself a violation of what I am delineating as the Jesus idea. The separate vision of a denomination *tends* to give to the individual who embraces it an ultimate, particularized status, even before God; as one of the older men in my boyhood church who admonished me because I was attending too many activities in the Methodist church: "Sometimes," he said, "I think that I am a Baptist first and a Christian second." In our moments of profoundest sobriety, there is clear recognition of the contradiction that is inherent in the concept of denominationalism as it is examined in the light of what for Christianity is the

Jesus idea. Inasmuch as the individual brings to his religious experience his context, it is perfectly natural and mandatory that he will enter his religious experience with his particular denominational frame of reference. That is the door through which he enters. In the encounter with God in the religious experience, however, the denominational frame of reference receives its true status, which is a *frame of reference,* without standing, as such, in the ultimate meaning of the experience itself. To make the frame of reference which is merely symbolic take on the life-giving character of the experience itself and thereby become binding as a principle of discrimination in the wider context of living and experiencing is to blaspheme against the experience itself. This, in my judgment, tends to undermine the integrity of the church as the promoter and inspirer of religious experience.

But when the church, even within the framework of the principle of discrimination inherent in denominationalism, further delimits itself in terms of class and race, it tends to become an instrument of violence to the religious experience. Here we come upon the shame of what is meant by the phrase of a certain minister in referring to the eleven o'clock hour on Sunday morning as "the great and sacred hour of segregation."

— *The Creative Encounter,* 139, 140–42

In an article in *The Atlantic Monthly,* Professor Toynbee has suggested the very real possibility that, if we are so foolish as to destroy our entire civilization and our own lives, then the creator of life could very easily make an ideal culture out of the ant. It is a most sobering thought. Again and again the human race has behaved as if it has some kind of monopoly on survival — and survival on its own terms, at that. The Church tends to foster this same notion. All the days of my life, I have heard men say that God is absolutely dependent upon the Church to spearhead His will and establish His true purposes

among men; if the Church fails, God is exhausted, and there
is no other means at His disposal. This seems to be essentially
unsound; even men are more resourceful than that. Once upon
a time, John remarked that if men were silent, then even the
rocks would cry aloud. Men may grow and develop into more
whole and complete beings, spreading all of life with a glory
that springs out of an increasing understanding of the meaning
and the possibilities of life; or they may become more and more
involved in their own devices, petty dreams, and unworthy ends
until, at last, the very processes which they have set in motion
blot them from the earth. If this should happen, or if it should
not, it must be remembered always that God is infinitely more
resourceful and creative than any expression of life, however
profound and exceptional that expression of life may be.

— *Deep Is the Hunger*, 38–39

•

Years ago I had made a tentative discovery when I preached
for the first time in the Methodist Church in my hometown
and, to my amazement, discovered that I had the same kind
of religious experience there that I had had in my own Baptist
Church. Now, in India, there was a redefining of that experience, only in a much more complex and subtle way. I had to
seek a means by which I could get to the essence of the religious
experience of Hinduism as I sat or stood or walked in a Hindu
temple where everything was foreign and new: the smells, the
altars, the flowers, the chanting — all of it was completely outside my universe of discourse. I had to find my way to the place
where I could stand side by side with a Hindu, a Buddhist, a
Moslem, and know that the authenticity of his experience was
identical with the essence and authenticity of my own. There
began to emerge a growing concept in my mind, which only
in recent years I have been able to state categorically, namely,
that the things that are true in any religious experience are to

be found in that religious experience precisely because they are true; they are not true simply because they are found in that religious experience. It is not the context that determines validity. On any road, around any turning, a man may come upon the burning bush and hear a voice say, "Take off your shoes because the place where you are now standing is a holy place, even though you did not know it before." I think that is the heartbeat of religious authority. Little did I dream that the discovery that I began to make in the Methodist Church in Daytona, Florida, as a young Baptist preacher, would move in a straight line to the Temple of the Fish Eye in Madura.

This is not to say that all religions are one and the same, but it is to say that the essence of religious experience is unique, comprehensible, and not delimiting.

— *With Head and Heart,* 120–21

Is the religious experience as defined uniquely Christian or is it more universal in character? If in the religious experience a man identifies Jesus rather than God as the other principal in his religious experience, then the *exclusive* character of the religious experience becomes undeniable. In my judgment this raises more questions than it solves because it places the most fundamental moment in the life of the individual at the disposal of only those persons who bring to the moment a certain body of formal beliefs. Such a position establishes on theological and metaphysical grounds a *principle of separateness* in the human family that paves the way for the promulgation in the world of a Cult of Inequality that puts man against man and group against group. If such a cult is rooted in an experience so profound, as the religious experience is, then the metaphysical purpose that such an experience generates becomes a banner under which all manner of brutality and human misery may march.

But if in the religious experience the other principal is God, who is sensed as Creator of life and Father of the human spirit, then at such a moment the individual stands on his intrinsic worthfulness as a human being and affirms in the integrity of the moment his solidarity with all mankind.

The character then of a social institution whose inspiration is rooted in its commitment to that kind of religious experience becomes more and more defined in activities, functions, social attitudes, that defy all class, group, or ethnic affiliation. The startling words of Jesus come to life again. "For whosoever shall do the will of my Father which is in heaven, the same is my brother, and sister, and mother" (Matthew 12:50).

— *The Creative Encounter*, 147–48

REASON FOR HOPE

There is a strange irony in the usual salutation, "Merry Christmas," when most of the people on this planet are thrown back upon themselves for food which they do not possess, for resources that have long since been exhausted, and for vitality which has already run its course. Nevertheless, the inescapable fact remains that Christmas symbolizes hope even at a moment when hope seems utterly fantastic. The raw materials of the Christmas mood are a newborn baby, a family, friendly animals, and labor. An endless process of births is the perpetual answer of life to the fact of death. It says that life keeps coming on, keeps seeking to fulfill itself, keeps affirming the margin of hope in the presence of desolation, pestilence, and despair. It is not an accident that the birth rate seems always to increase during times of war, when the formal processes of man are engaged in the destruction of others. Welling up out of the depths of vast vitality, there is something at work that is more authentic than

the formal discursive design of the human mind. As long as this
is true ultimately, despair about the human race is groundless.

— Deep Is the Hunger, 38

Madonna and Child

During the season of Christmas in many art galleries, in count-
less homes and churches, and on myriad Christmas cards, there
will be scenes picturing the Madonna and Child. There is
a sense in which the Madonna and Child experience is not
the exclusive possession of any faith or any race. This is not
to gainsay, to underestimate, or to speak irreverently of the
far-reaching significance of the Madonna in Christianity, particularly in Roman Catholicism. But it is to point out the fact
that the Madonna and Child both in art and religion is a recognition of the universality of the experience of motherhood as an
expression of the creative and redemptive principle of life. It affirms the constancy of the idea that life is dynamic and alive —
that death as the final consummation of life is an illusion.

The limitless resources of life are at the disposal of the creative impulse that fulfills itself most intimately and profoundly
in the experience of the birth of a child. Here the mother
becomes one with the moving energy of existence — in the
experience of birth there is neither time, nor space, nor indi-
viduality, nor private personal existence — she is absorbed in a
vast creative moment upon which the continuity of the race is
dependent. The experience itself knows no race, no culture, no
language — it is the trysting place of woman and the Eternal.

The Madonna and Child in Christianity is profoundly rooted
in this background of universality. Specifically, it dramatizes the
birth of a Jewish baby, under unique circumstances, calling attention to a destiny in which the whole human race is involved.
For many to whom he is the Savior of mankind, no claim as
to his origin is too great or too lofty. Here is the culmination

of a vast expectancy and the fulfillment of a desperate need. Through the ages the message of him whose coming is celebrated at Christmastime says again and again through artists, through liturgy, through music, through the written and spoken word, through great devotion and heroic sacrifice, that the destiny of man on earth is a good and common destiny — that however dark the moment or the days may be, the redemptive impulse of God is ever present in human life.

But there is something more. The Madonna and Child conception suggests that the growing edge of human life, the hope of every generation, is in the birth of the child. The stirring of the child in the womb is the perennial sign of man's attack on bigotry, blindness, prejudice, greed, hate, and all the host of diseases that make of man's life a nightmare and a holocaust.

The Birth of the Child in China, Japan, the Philippines, Russia, India, America, and all over the world, is the breathless moment like the stillness of absolute motion, when something new, fresh, whole, may be ushered into the nations that will be the rallying point for the whole human race to move in solid phalanx into the city of God, into the Kingdom of Heaven on the earth. . . .　　　　　 — *The Mood of Christmas*, 15–16

Christmas Is Waiting to Be Born

Where refugees seek deliverance that never comes,
And the heart consumes itself, if it would live,
Where little children age before their time,
And life wears down the edges of the mind,
Where the old man sits with mind grown cold,
While bones and sinew, blood and cell, go slowly down to
　　death,
Where fear companions each day's life,
And Perfect Love seems long delayed.

CHRISTMAS IS WAITING TO BE BORN:
In you, in me, in all mankind.

— The Mood of Christmas, 21

The Work of Christmas

When the song of the angels is stilled,
When the star in the sky is gone,
When the kings and princes are home,
When the shepherds are back with their flock,
The work of Christmas begins:
  To find the lost,
  To heal the broken,
  To feed the hungry,
  To release the prisoner,
  To rebuild the nations,
  To bring peace among brothers,
  To make music in the heart.

— The Mood of Christmas, 23

The Valley of Death

Though I walk through the Valley of the Shadow of Death,
I will fear no evil.

"Though I walk through the Valley of the Shadow." My journey through the Valley of the Shadow of Death may be hurried, swift. If so, this fact may reduce my fear, my anxiety. The time interval may be so short, and so much may happen, that fear does not have a chance at me. This lack of fear occurs with acute illness sometimes or with exposure to sudden danger. But if the illness is long drawn out and there is time for the gradual unfolding to the real meaning of my condition, then I seem to be more completely at the disposal of all kinds of fears as well as of fear itself. Thus I *walk* through the Valley of the Shadow.

"The Valley of the Shadow of Death." Is there some important difference between the valley of death and the Valley of the Shadow of Death? There is something which seems more deeply sinister about the Valley of the Shadow. There is the sense of impending danger, of threat. It is the war of nerves which life seems to be waging. The ax does not fall. I do not see the ax but always there is squarely across my path, the Shadow of the Ax. Such extended experiences shatter the nerves and tend to demoralize the life. Fear of this quality seems completely destructive.

"I will fear no evil." When I *walk* through the *valley* of the *shadow* of death, I will fear no evil because God is with me. And His Presence makes the difference, because it cancels out the threatening element of the threat, the evil element of evil. Of course I may linger, or I may die; I may suffer acutely, or all my days may rest upon an undercurrent of muted agony. I shall not be overcome; God is with me. My awareness of God's Presence may sound like magic, it may seem to some to be the merest childlike superstition, but it meets my need and is at once the source of my comfort and the heart of my peace.

> Though I walk through the Valley of the Shadow of Death,
> I will fear no evil.

— *Meditations of the Heart,* 185–86

•

The religious experiences of the slave were rich and full because his avenues of emotional expression were definitely limited and circumscribed. His religious aspirations were expressed in many songs delineating varying aspects of his desires. The other-worldly hope looms large, and this of course is not strange; the other-worldly hope is always available when groups of people

find themselves completely frustrated in the present. When all
hope for release in this world seems unrealistic and groundless,
the heart turns to a way of escape beyond the present order.
The options are very few for those who are thus circumstanced.
Their belief in God leads quite definitely to a position that fixes
their hope on deliverance beyond the grave. What a plaintive
cry are these words:

> Don't leave me, Lord
> Don't leave me behin'.

There is desolation, fear, loneliness, but hope, at once desperate
and profound!   —*Deep River,* 29–30

The Glad Surprise

There is ever something compelling and exhilarating about the
glad surprise. The emphasis is upon *glad.* There are surprises
that are shocking, startling, frightening, and bewildering. But
the glad surprise is something different from all of these. It carries with it the element of elation, of life, of something over
and beyond the surprise itself. The experience itself comes at
many levels: the simple joy that comes when one discovers that
the balance in the bank is larger than the personal record indicated — and there is no error in accounting; the realization that
one does not have his doorkey — the hour is late and everyone is asleep — but someone very thoughtfully left the latch off,
"just in case"; the dreaded meeting in a conference to work out
some problems of misunderstanding, and things are adjusted
without the emotional lacerations anticipated; the report from
the doctor's examination that all is well, when one was sure
that the physical picture was very serious indeed. All of these
surprises are glad!

There is a deeper meaning in the concept of the glad surprise.
This meaning has to do with the very ground and foundation

of hope about the nature of life itself. The manifestation of this quality in the world about us can best be witnessed in the coming of spring. It is ever a new thing, a glad surprise, the stirring of life at the end of winter. One day there seems to be no sign of life and then almost overnight, swelling buds, delicate blooms, blades of grass, bugs, insects — an entire world of newness everywhere. It is the glad surprise at the end of winter. Often the same experience comes at the end of a long tunnel of tragedy and tribulation. It is as if a man stumbling in the darkness, having lost his way, finds that the spot at which he falls is the foot of a stairway that leads from darkness into light. Such is the glad surprise. This is what Easter means in the experience of the race. This is the resurrection! It is the announcement that life cannot ultimately be conquered by death, that there is no road that is at last swallowed up in an ultimate darkness, that there is strength added when the labors increase, that multiplied peace matches multiplied trials, that life is bottomed by the glad surprise. Take courage, therefore:

> When we have exhausted our store of endurance,
> When our strength has failed ere the day is half done,
> When we reach the end of our hoarded resources,
> Our Father's full giving is only begun.

> — *Meditations of the Heart,* 108–10

Chapter 2

The Hunger for Community

The sense of Oneness that comes from religious experience is understood by Thurman to be the reality that God intends for creation. Religious experience discloses the underlying unity of reality and God's desire that life be lived in resonance with such unity. The term Howard Thurman most frequently uses to characterize this unity is "community."

Not only is community the given character of reality, but life is in process toward manifesting this goal. Community is the telos (end purpose) of life. This leads Thurman to conclude that the ultimate destiny of humanity is good. Anything that stands against such community cannot ultimately prevail. And since, as he says, "the contradictions of life are not final," community will be the last word.

Howard Thurman believes that nature can teach humanity about living in harmony. Yes, nature has its excesses. Death occurs on a monumental scale. But nature also manifests a complex network of interrelationships. Whether by studying the life of the cell, the behavior of pets, or the research of botanists and biologists, Thurman is instructed about how community functions. Each observation and investigation yields insights on how community and the urge for community are imprinted in every expression of life. This, he believes, is God's signature on everything in creation.

Community also functions as humanity's home. We are created for *community. We are born into community (i.e., the family) and depend upon it for survival. We are nurtured by community. This does not deny that people experience abandonment and abuse. But such experiences are a betrayal of the stronger and more persistent urge for care and whole-making. Community is a gift of God. We honor this gift when we live in community with respect and care for its members and all creation. Stewardship of community is thus a fundamental spiritual discipline.*

So many breakdowns in relationships among humans result from the urge to dominate others. The most blatant division within societies is between the privileged and the disinherited. As noted in the introduction, Thurman devoted much of his vocation to addressing the cultural and religious sickness of racism in America. Racism, for Thurman, is primarily a spiritual crisis requiring a spiritual antidote. He relies upon the witness of Jesus for discovering the love-ethic as the healing antidote. Jesus' example provides the means by which freedom and reconciliation are possible.

Thurman believes that despite the constant conflicts of existence, community can be experienced in time and space. That experience may last only a season, but that season reassures and readies us for the journey ahead. If one is fixated on experiencing the reconciled community *that stays in harmonious relationship once and forever, then one is doomed to frustration and disappointment. However, to be committed to* the reconciling community *is to know joy, renewal, and a sense of ultimate fulfillment. Frustration and disappointment remain, but they do not become the dominant emotions. Thurman is convinced that the forces of love, cooperation, right relationship, respect, and nurture will prevail — perhaps not* in *one's lifetime, but certainly* for *lifetimes to come.*

THE NATURE OF NATURE

The literal fact of the underlying unity of life seems to be established beyond doubt. It manifests itself in the basic structural patterns of nature and provides the precious clue to the investigation and interpretation of the external world of man. At any point in time and space one may come upon the door that opens into the central place where the building blocks of existence are always being manufactured. True, man has not been able to decipher all the codes in their highly complex variations, but he is ever on the scent.

If life has been fashioned out of a fundamental unity and ground, and if it has developed within such a structure, then it is not to be wondered at that the interest in and concern for wholeness should be part of the conscious intent of life, more basic than any particular conscious tendency toward fragmentation. Every expression of life is trying to experience itself. For a form of life to experience itself it must actualize its own unique potential. In so doing it experiences in miniature the fundamental unity out of which it comes.

— Disciplines of the Spirit, 104

In human society, the experience of community, or realized potential, is rooted in life itself because the intuitive human urge for community reflects a characteristic of all life. In the total panorama of the external world of nature, there seems to be a pattern of structural dependability and continuity, or what may be called an inner logic, that manifests itself in forms, organizational schemes, and in a wide variety of time-space arrangements. The most striking pattern of all is that there seems to be affinity between the human mind and all external forms, a fact that makes an understanding of the world possible for the mind.

The religious basis for such an interpretation of community is the affirmation, which to me is categorical, that the Mind of God realizes Itself in *time*, and that there are observable patterns or sequences in all creation. Thus God is thought of as Creator. From this point of view, all time-space manifestations of substance — in short, all things, even existence itself — are regarded as the Mind of God coming to *Itself* in time and space. This is evident in history and in nature. Existence itself is construed as divine activity. There seems to be a principle of rationality in all existence, and the significance of this can be found in the order of life. True, what seems to be a principle of rationality as expressed in observable order in life may be a limitation of mind itself. Yet it is this assumption of inherent logic in the functioning of the mind that makes comprehension of the external world possible.

— The Search for Common Ground, 5

The most fundamental characteristic of life is its search for nourishment. If this be true, then the individual in his experience with commitment is not introducing into the picture an element that is foreign or unknown to the basis of life. Rather, in the basic conditions of its life the organism knows in a very profound and far-reaching way the discipline of commitment. Its whole existence depends upon the singleness of this kind of demand — the demand for food, for survival.

Let us examine this further. Life is *alive;* this is its abiding quality as long as it prevails at all. The word "life" is synonymous with vitality. Of course we are aware that individual forms of life around us are living things. In your own household you know that your cat, or dog, or canary, or rosebush, are alive. You know that your child, or husband, or wife, or friend, are alive as you relate to them within a living context. This is obvious. We are so conscious of the fact of each individual expression of life about us that the simplest and most wonderful fact of all is passed by. And what is that? The fact that life itself is alive, has the persistent trait of living — that any and all living things continue to survive as long as that essential vitality is available to them.   — *Disciplines of the Spirit,* 14

•

I am convinced that there is a ground of unity between animals and man of which any oral communication is but symbolic or vehicular. The oral communication must be of such sounds that they unlock the door between. How this is done we do not know. The notion that man is the higher animal and all others are lower, the development of elaborate self-consciousness in man, the ability to think reflectively that is a use of the mind that gives it the sense of living its own life apart from the body — all of these and kindred ideas have erected a great wall between man and other animals. The sense of separateness from the rest of nature is so marked that man tends to see himself as being over against nature. In defense of this conceit, various dogmas and even theologies have been developed. My point is not that the sense of separateness is not authentic but merely that it is not absolute. Life is always seeking to realize itself in myriad forms and patterns of manifestation. These forms and manifestations include the organic structure as well as diffused consciousness or awareness at its most elemental level and self-consciousness in its profoundest expression.

Fear keeps the doors between sealed. It is a basic response to threat. Over so many years men and animals have lived essentially apart from each other and the predatory instinct, particularly among men, has been so crucial in their survival that any notion of community that moves out beyond the protective enclosure is fatuous and illusory. But where there is deliberate acceptance between men and animals, a fresh possibility of enlarged meaning for each emerges. I suspect that under such circumstances even the potential of each life undergoes a radical expansion. Once the acceptance has taken place, even ancient enmity begins to give way and new meanings emerge.   — *The Search for Common Ground*, 62–63

Man cannot long separate himself from nature without withering as a cut rose in a vase. One of the deceptive aspects of mind in man is to give him the illusion of being distinct from and over against but not a part of nature. It is but a single leap thus to regard nature as being so completely other than himself that he may exploit it, plunder it, and rape it with impunity.

This we see all around us in the modern world. Our atmosphere is polluted, our streams are poisoned, our hills are denuded, wild life is increasingly exterminated, while more and more man becomes an alien on the earth and a fouler of his own nest. The price that is being exacted for this is a deep sense of isolation, of being rootless and a vagabond. Often I have surmised that this condition is more responsible for what seems to be the phenomenal increase in mental and emotional disturbances in modern life than the pressures — economic, social, and political — that abound on every hand. The collective psyche shrieks with the agony that it feels as a part of the death cry of a pillaged nature.

                    — *The Search for Common Ground*, 83–84

•

Through all of this I was on my own scent. The sacred and the secular were aspects of a single reality, a single meaning. At no point could a line of separation be drawn. At long last it seems to me that the customary distinction between religion and life is a specious one. As I have felt my way back through the twists and turns of my own journey over the years, every facet of my way *belongs,* inherently. There is not a single experience that does not have a secret door opening out on the panorama of all my past; and I am confident that this is also true of my future. Even the most trivial event provides some clue of meaning to the broad expanse of the road over which I have already come. It points the way to that which may yet await me around some turn in the road ahead. "Nothing walks with aimless feet" is not to say that I am bound and held fast by the mystery of a kismet or even a predestination. But it is to say that all life, indeed all experience, is heavy with meaning, with particular significance.   — *With Head and Heart,* 268

It is the fundamental realization of the notion that life is its own restraint that sustained the slave in his darkest days, and gave him an elemental vigor that expressed itself in a deep optimism arising out of the pessimism of life. He picks up the searching words of Jeremiah and sings his affirmation, "There is a balm in Gilead!" Of course there are those who may say that this is merely a defense mechanism, likened unto the mood of a man in prison who thanks God that he is there; for if he were not, he might be hit by a stray bullet. Such reflections regard this mood as a defense mechanism, which becomes a substitute for action that would relieve the pressure. The only answer to this is that there would have been no survival in this philosophy for the Negro if it were merely a mechanism of sheer defense.

The second insight here is that the contradictions of life are not in themselves either final or ultimate. This points up the basic difference between pessimism and optimism. The pessimist appraises the facts of experience, and on their face value is constrained to pass a final judgment on them. If there are contradictions between good and evil — between that which makes for peace and that which makes for turbulence — then these contradictions are regarded from this point of view as being in themselves ultimate and final; and because they are ultimate, inescapable, and therefore binding. Back of such a view is the conception that life in essence is fixed, finished, unchanging. Man is caught in the agonizing grip of inevitables; and whatever may be his chance or circumstantial assignment, all his alternatives are reduced to zero. For the man in power this is a happy philosophy. All notions of social superiority based on the elevation of a principle of racial inequality lifted to the dimension of a law of life, find their nourishment here. They state in bold terms that the God of the universe is basically partial, immoral or amoral; or, from the point of view of the underprivileged by birth or election, God is demoniacal. This undermines all hope for the oppressed, and if it is embraced gives them no sense of the future that is different from the experience of the past. The structure of the universe is stacked against them, and they may die in ultimate defiance of it, but their death will be but a futile gesture, bringing havoc to all who survive the relentless logic of such abiding fatalism.

But if perchance the contradictions of life are not ultimate, then there is always the growing edge of hope in the midst of the most barren and most tragic circumstances. It is a complete renunciation of the thoroughgoing dualism of the point of view just discussed. It is a matter of supreme significance that men are never quite robbed of all hope. There is something present in the spirit of man, sometimes even taking the form of great arrogance, sometimes quietly nourishing the springs of resistance to a great tyranny — there is something in the spirit of man that knows that the dualism, however apparently binding, runs out, exhausts itself, and leaves a core of assurance that the ultimate destiny of man is good. This becomes the raw material of all hope, and is one of the tap-roots of religious faith for the human spirit. When it applies to the individual and becomes the norm of human relationships, a new sense of the ethical significance of life becomes manifest. Just as no man

is ever quite willing — protestations to the contrary notwith-
standing — to give himself up, so we are under judgment not to
give each other up. The root of this judgment is found in the
fact that deep within us is the conviction that man's destiny is
a good destiny. To illustrate. For a period — how long we do
not know but certainly ever since the memory of man became
self-conscious — there has been war among men. Yet in times of
even temporary cessation from struggle, or in times of greatest
conflict, the dream of peace continues to nourish the hope of the
race. This dream persists, even though we do not know what
peace on earth would be like because it has never been experienced. We continue to hope against all evidence to the contrary,
because that hope is fed by a conviction deeper than the processes of thought that the destiny of man is good. It is this spirit
that has been captured by the spiritual. Yes, *"There is a balm in
Gilead to heal the sin-sick soul."* The day that this conviction
leaves the spirit of man, his moment on the earth is over, and
the last fond hope of the race perishes from the earth forever,
and a lonely God languishes while before Him His dreams go
silently to dust.   — *Deep River,* 62–65

COMMUNITY AS CRUCIBLE

The profoundest disclosure in the religious experience is the
awareness that the individual is not alone. What he discovers as
being true and valid for himself must at last be a universal experience, or else it ultimately loses all of its personal significance.
His experience is personal, private, but in no sense exclusive.
All of the vision of God and holiness which he experiences, he
must achieve in the context of the social situation by which his
day-by-day life is defined. What is disclosed in his religious experience he must define in community. That which God shareth
with him, he must inspire his fellows to seek for themselves.

He is dedicated therefore to the removing of all barriers which block or frustrate this possibility in the world. He is under judgment to make a highway for the Lord in the hearts and in the market place of his fellows. Through his living men must find it a reasonable thing to trust Him and to trust one another and therefore to be brought nearer to the great sacramental moment when they too are exposed to the love of God at a point in them beyond the evil and the good....

The logic of the kind of religious experience that we have been describing points toward an individual-centered culture pattern. If in something as significant as the religious experience the individual personality is the crucial point of reference, not because of who the individual is, or what the individual is, or the shape of his head, or the color of his eyebrows, then it follows that a society that is personality-centered would provide a climate predisposed to religious experience and all that it indicates for the enrichment and meaning of life.

—*The Creative Encounter,* 123–24, 129–30

The place to look for the emergence of community in human life is in the primary social unit, the family. It is here that the child first becomes aware of himself as a person. It has often been said that a child is not born human but becomes human only in a human situation or context. I take this to mean that in the intimacy of the family the profound process of the unfolding of potential is set in motion. The goal of fulfillment appears on the far horizon and persists as the pull of the long-timed emotion of the ideal. The child may fail both within and without, but against that failure something wars, always pushing, always making its claim felt. It is the claim of the building blocks, the built-in demand of the mind, the insistence of the organism, the upward push of the racial memory, the glow of the prophets' demand and the dream of the seer; it is what in religion is often called the will of God as touching the life of man.

What happens if in the life of the child there is in the family no pivotal point around which positive self-awareness emerges? The child is apt to become permanently crippled. This period of the child is also characterized as a time of innocence. In that sense there is the recapitulation of the story of the race as found in the various creation myths or query stories. For the child, very important things are happening in his organism, for the track is being laid for the life journey of the body. In terms of community, this means that if the child is forced by the circumstances of his life to cope with his environment as if he were an adult, his very nervous system becomes enraged and an utter sense of alienation is apt to become the style of his life. Because he is rejected by life he begins to reject himself. The process of withdrawal and alienation begins its deadly operation before the child has any tools for assessing or interpreting what is happening to him. As an unconscious windbreak against this kind of communal suicide, provisions are made within the scope of the culture for giving children an early sense of belonging to the group as a whole and to a primary group within the larger relationships that give character to the total society.

— *The Search for Common Ground*, 81–82

•

My chief concern [while at Shantiniketan University in India] was to have some time with Dr. Singh, who was the head of the division of Oriental studies in the university. One glorious morning we sat on the floor in searching conversation about the life of the spirit, Hinduism, Buddhism, and Christianity. When lunchtime came, I had to keep an appointment with some students. Getting up from the floor, massaging my usual charley horse, I looked at him.

He remarked, "I see you are chuckling."

I replied that he was doing the same. "Perhaps we are reacting to the same thing," I said.

"Suppose you tell me first," he remarked.

I said we had spent the entire morning sparring for position — "you from behind your Hindu breastwork, and I from behind my Christian embattlement. Now and then, we step out from that protection, draw a bead on each other, then retreat."

"You are right. When we come back this afternoon, let us be wiser than that."

That afternoon I had the most primary, naked fusing of total religious experience with another human being of which I have ever been capable. It was as if we had stepped out of social, political, cultural frames of reference, and allowed two human spirits to unite on a ground of reality that was unmarked by separateness and differences. This was a watershed of experience in my life. We had become a part of each other even as we remained essentially individual. I was able to stand secure in my place and enter into his place without diminishing myself or threatening him.   — *With Head and Heart,* 129

Fellowship Church was a unique idea, fresh, untried. There were no precedents and no traditions to aid in structuring the present or gauging the future. Yet Sue and I knew that all our accumulated experiences of the past had given us two crucial gifts for this undertaking: a profound conviction that meaningful and creative experiences between peoples can be more compelling than all the ideas, concepts, faiths, fears, ideologies, and prejudices that divide them; and absolute faith that if such experiences can be multiplied and sustained over a time interval of sufficient duration *any* barrier that separates one person from another can be undermined and eliminated. We were sure that the ground of such meaningful experiences could be provided by the widest possible associations around common interest and common concerns.   — *With Head and Heart,* 148

If I Ascend up into Heaven, Thou Art There!
[Psalm 139:8]

If I ascend up into heaven, Thou art there!
    When my joy overflows and
    No words contain it;
    When the thing I sought was lost
    Only to reappear within the hollow of my hand;
    When the day seems interminable
    But at eventide the burdens lift
    And weariness is a far-off memory;
    When there opens before the vista of the mind
    The wonder of new regions, far-off places;
    When the gentle touch of a loved one
    Makes music heard only by the listening heart;
    When the doctor's word is the final word
    And deep within the hidden places of the life
    Healing waters stir, bringing wholeness in their wake —
    When the wanderer comes home
    And the wayward finds peace in the ancient fireside —
    When from the ashes of old dreams
    The fires of a new life are kindled —
    Thou art there!

If I make my bed in hell — behold
    When night remains night
    And darkness deepens;
    When the evilness of evil is unrelieved
    And utter desolation makes mockery
    Of all that was true and good;
    When the open door of refuge
    Closes in my face
    And to turn back is of no avail;
    When the firm grip of sanity trembles

And all balances tilt, leaving
The mind tortured and crazed;
When all around, worlds crash
And winds blow torrid
Over the parched and wasted
Places of my spirit;
When sin multiplies itself
Until at last all goodness
Seems swallowed up and devoured;
When the chuckle of death
Is the only sound to be heard in the land,
Thou art there!

If I make my bed in hell . . .
If I ascend up into heaven . . .
    Behold!

— The Inward Journey, 147–48

THE HOUNDS OF HELL

One may lose fear also by a sense of being a part of a company of people who share the same concerns and are conscious of participating in the same collective destiny. This is an additional form that the feeling of community inspires. A strange and wonderful courage often comes into a man's life when he shares a commitment to something that is more important than whether he himself lives or dies. It is the discovery of the dynamic character of life itself. This may not be a conscious act as far as the rationale for it is concerned. It *is* a discovery of the conditions under which fresh resources of energy are available. When a person is able to place at the disposal of a single end, goal, or purpose the resources of his life, his strength is magnified a hundredfold or even a thousandfold. He relaxes his hold upon his own physical existence because he is caught up in the kind of enlarged consciousness or expanded awareness that is triggered by the commitment that his life becomes important only in terms that fulfill the inscrutable demands of the commitment. Such an experience is spiritual; yea, it is religious. In such a moment a man has the feeling that he is totally encompassed, totally alive, and more completely himself than he has ever been before. Under such a circumstance, even death is a little thing. This is the reason why there is a kind of fervor — not hysteria but a kind of fervor — that so often illumines the countenances of those who are peacefully demonstrating in the face of the threat of violence. I recognize that there may be mass hysteria into which people are caught up and the ability to stick by one's witness under duress may be created out of hostility and an overriding anger. But there is another and vaster possibility which has made itself manifest here and there during these fateful days: a deep spiritual awareness that one's life is in vital touch with the Source of Being that holds and makes secure against all that destroys and lays waste.

— *The Luminous Darkness*, 57–58

•

> I got wings,
> You got wings,
> All God's children got wings.

The setting of this spiritual is very dramatic. The slave had often heard his master's minister talk about heaven, the final abode of the righteous. Naturally the master regarded himself as fitting into that category. On the other hand the slave knew that *he* too was going to heaven. He reasoned, "There must be two separate heavens — no, this could not be true, because there is only one God. God cannot be divided in this way. I have it! I am having my hell now — when I die I shall have my heaven.

The master is having his heaven now; when he dies he will have his hell."

The next day, chopping cotton beneath the torrid skies, the slave said to his mate —

> I got shoes,
> You got shoes,
> All God's children got shoes.
> When we get to Heaven
> We're goin' to put on our shoes
> An' shout all over God's Heaven.
> Heaven! Heaven!

Then looking up to the big house where the master lived, he said:

> But everybody talking 'bout Heaven
> Ain't going there.

This is one of the authentic songs of protest. It was sung in anticipation of a time that even yet has not fully come — a time when there shall be no slave row in the church, no gallery set aside for the slave, no special place, no segregation, no badge of racial and social stigma, but complete freedom of movement. Even at that far-off moment in the past, these early singers put their fingers on the most vulnerable spot in Christianity and democracy. The wide, free range of his spirit sent him in his song beyond all barriers. In God's presence at least there would be freedom; slavery is no part of the purpose or the plan of God. Man, therefore, is the great enemy of man. This is the mood of that song.

But there is a further problem here of critical, ethical import. The age-old technique by which the weak have survived in the midst of the strong is to fool the strong. Deception, hypocrisy, lying, become the mechanism by which the weak protect themselves from the strong. . . .

The ethical question here raised has to do with the issue of compromise. If the choice is between annihilation and survival, does that mean that deception and hypocrisy take on a moral quality that drains them of their toxin? If this is true, then perhaps there was no moral issue in the mind from the beginning. It is one of the great spiritual problems of Christianity in America that it has tolerated such injustices between Negroes and Caucasians, for instance; that in this area of human relations its moral imperative has been greatly weakened. It is for this reason that many people all over the world feel that Christianity is weakest when it is brought face to face with the color bar.

—*Deep River*, 47–48, 49–50

•

The setting for hate often begins in situations where there are contacts without fellowship. That is, contacts that are devoid of the simple overtones of warmth, fellow-feeling, and genuineness. There is some region in every man that listens for the sound of the genuine in other men. But where there is contact that is stripped of fellow-feeling, the sound cannot come through and the will to listen for it is not manifest. What happens behind the walls of segregation when the reaction to segregation is positive resentment and bitterness? I am not unmindful that there can be and often is an abundance of sentimentality masquerading under the cloak of fellowship. I am remembering also that all through the years there have been isolated experiences of genuine fellowship. Even in the South the walls of segregation were sometimes transcended and a person behind the walls listened for and heard the sound of the genuine in the person on the other side. But this is rare. . . .

Contacts without fellowship tend to express themselves in unsympathetic understanding. To be sure, there is understanding of a certain kind, but it is without the healing and reinforcement of personality. The energy and spirit of the persons involved are not available to each other. It is like the experience of going to a man's office to be interviewed for a job. In that stripping moment before being seated, when the full gaze of the other person is focused upon you, suddenly you wonder if your tie is crooked, or if one of the buttons on your shirt is missing, but you dare not look to find out. In such a penetrating, incisive, cold understanding there is no cushion to absorb limitations or to provide extenuating circumstances for protection. . . .

Unsympathetic understanding is very easily activated into ill will. It may be quite an unconscious step or movement of the spirit. It may be a general or pervasive mood which influences the character of casual encounters or it may inform, quite intentionally, the pointed, face-to-face encounter. It breeds suspicion and inspires many little acts of no-faith. It creates an all-encompassing climate. This unsympathetic understanding may make the Negro say, "No white man can be trusted," or it may make the white person say, "All Negroes are liars and thieves." It makes the areas of contact become a no man's land where men move around as shadows in a world of shadows. . . .

There is a dynamic quality in the residue which points up the paradox of hate. Hatred may become a foundation upon which the personality stands in an effort to establish a dreadful emotional security. It is possible for a personal significance to emerge on the other side of hate that becomes a form of self-validation. As such it is so intensely personal and private that it becomes a fortress for the ego structure. For a limited and on occasion extended time interval the individual seems to be impregnable. When this happens the very hatred itself becomes an internal rallying center for the personality. The energy generated may be regarded as the strength of a kind of neurosis. Surplus energy is created and placed at the disposal of the individual's needs and ends. The whole personality seems

to be alerted. All kinds of supports for implementing one's af-
firmed or confirmed position are seized upon. A strange new
cunning possesses the mind, and every opportunity for taking
advantage, for defeating, for striking out against the enemy is
revealed in clear perspective. An amazing quality of endurance
emerges. It must never be forgotten that hate has an endurance
capability in what it may inspire the human spirit to suffer and
to sustain....

Hate also wills the nonexistence of another human being. It
is not the same as willing the destruction of another person;
such is often the aim of bitterness and hostility. Hate is at another and a more profound level; it undermines the very being
of the other by affirming his nonexistence and accepting this affirmation as true and authentic. It is a withdrawal of sanction
of the other as existing. The person is not destroyed, for this
would be to acknowledge his existence, but it is to say that he
is not there. Of course this is a delusion, but it may be extremely
functional in behavior. This is refined evil.

— *The Luminous Darkness*, 38–39, 39–40,
40–41, 44–45, 45–46

RACE AS CRISIS

When I was a boy I earned money in the fall of the year by
raking leaves in the yard of a white family. I did this in the afternoon, after school. In this family there was a little girl about six
or seven years old. She delighted in following me around the
yard as I worked. One of her insistences was to scatter the piles
of leaves in order to find a particular shape to show me. Each
time it meant that I had to do my raking all over again. Despite
my urging she refused to stop what she was doing. Finally I told
her that I would report her to her father when he came home.
This was a real threat to her because she stood in great fear of

her father. She stopped, looked at me in anger, took a straight pin out of her pinafore, ran up to me and stuck me with the pin on the back of my hand. I pulled back my hand and exclaimed, "Ouch! Have you lost your mind?" Whereupon she said in utter astonishment, "That did not hurt you — you can't feel."

In other words, I was not human, nor was I even a creature capable of feeling pain. Manifestly this is an extreme position, but it indicates the social and psychological climate in which it would be possible for a little girl to grow up in a Christian family with such a spontaneous attitude toward other human beings. Segregation guarantees such inhumaneness and throws wide the door for a complete range of socially irresponsible behavior.   — *The Luminous Darkness*, 7–8

•

If the religious experience is genuine and in it the individual has an assurance of communion with God — this too has to fit into the facts of his life as he knows them. The insistent fact is that his life, as he himself knows it, does not merit such fellowship. If he experiences it without merit, then there is present, in the encounter, a gratuitous element or grace. If the experience is characterized by grace, then God is acting arbitrarily and from within a totality that is not available to the individual himself. Hence God sees something in the individual of which the individual himself is scarcely aware. This marks the individual off from his fellows and singles him out for special favor. Unless the individual is able constantly to identify himself with his fellows even in the presence of God, he will vitiate his insights so that what is good in him at last becomes evil in its very uniqueness. But if he maintains his sense of identity with his fellows, then what he is experiencing or experiences, all men everywhere stand in immediate or indirect candidacy to experience, and a part of his response to God is the shared knowledge of God's availability to all. Once again we see how the fight with pride becomes personal. The religious experience must belong *to* life and therefore be the subject of understanding.

— *The Creative Encounter,* 58–60

It is unspeakably ironical that the tremendous doctrine of grace may become a part of the supporting ground for racial and religious bigotry. Thus a man may carry the Gospel to an "outsider" with the hope and the fervent prayer that he may be helped into the way of grace and salvation. To that end he may sacrifice his substance, his status, even his life because his identification with the outsider's need is so demanding. Always, then, such a man can identify with the other's needs, predicament, and context without ever identifying with the man himself. The whole world can be saved, redeemed, and at the same time, the true relation between the giver and the receiver remain untouched, uninfluenced. To be specific: because a man is a Christian is no indication to me what his attitude may be toward me in any given circumstance.

It is not to be understood that the evangelical and the missionary impact tends to have no influence on the true relationship between people as people. It is to be understood that the curious distortion or corruption of the doctrine of grace supports a social attitude that is completely foreign to the mood and the spirit of the doctrine itself. Consequently, it is entirely possible that I, for instance, can work for the redemption of the souls of people, help them in their need in many critical ways, while at the same time keep them out of my neighborhood, out of my school, and out of my local church. And all of this with no apparent conflict in values or disturbance of conscience.

When a white person accepts the fact and the status of segregation he can carry on the normal intercourse of his life without being aware of it. In many superficial ways he may remain unaffected by it. He can live his entire life in a thousand communities all over the country and have no primary contact with Negroes. He can be secure in his own feeling of superiority, unchallenged. Or, as has been suggested, he can exercise his good will within the limitations vouched safe to him by his acceptance of the white person's status within the accepted pattern. But whether the acceptance is deliberate or indifferent, he becomes the party to a monstrous evil executed in his name and maintained in his behalf. The responsibility for the social decay and defiling of the spirit is inescapable, acknowledged or unacknowledged. For segregation is a sickness and no one who lives in its reach can claim or expect immunity. It makes men dishonest by forcing them to call an evil thing good; it makes them discourteous and rude when it is contrary to their temperaments and sense of values to be so.

— *The Luminous Darkness*, 63–65

•

The burden of being black and the burden of being white is so heavy that it is rare in our society to experience oneself as a human being. It may be, I do not know, that to experience oneself as a human being is one with experiencing one's fellows as human beings. Precisely what does it mean to experience oneself as a human being? In the first place, it means that the individual must have a sense of kinship to life that transcends and goes beyond the immediate kinship of family or the organic kinship that binds him ethnically or "racially" or nationally. He has to feel that he belongs to his total environment. He has a sense of being an essential part of the structural relationship that exists between him and all other men, and between him, all other men, and the total external environment. As a human being, then, he belongs to life and the whole kingdom of life that includes all that lives and perhaps, also, all that has ever lived. In other words, he sees himself as a part of a continuing, breathing, living existence. To be a human being, then, is to be essentially alive in a living world. — *The Luminous Darkness*, 94

On one of our visits to Daytona Beach I was eager to show my daughters some of my early haunts. We sauntered down the long street from the church to the riverfront. This had been the path of the procession to the baptismal ceremony in the Halifax River, which I had often described to them. We stopped here and there as I noted the changes that had taken place since that far-off time. At length we passed the playground of one of the white public schools. As soon as Olive and Anne saw the swings, they jumped for joy. "Look, Daddy, let's go over and swing!" This was the inescapable moment of truth that every black parent in America must face soon or late. What do you say to your child at the critical moment of primary encounter?

"You can't swing in those swings"

"Why?"

"When we get home and have some cold lemonade I will tell you." When we were home again, and had had our lemonade, Anne pressed for the answer. "We are home now, Daddy. Tell us."

I said, "It is against the law for us to use those swings, even though it is a public school. At present, only white children can play there. But it takes the state legislature, the courts, the sheriffs and policemen, the white churches, the mayors, the banks and businesses, and the majority of white people in the state of Florida — it takes all these to keep two little black girls from swinging in those swings. That is how important you are! Never forget, the estimate of your own importance and self-worth can be judged by how many weapons and how much power people are willing to use to control you and keep you in the place they have assigned to you. You are two very important little girls. Your presence can threaten the entire state of Florida."   — *With Head and Heart, 97*

If being Christian does not demand that all Christians love each other and thereby become deeply engaged in experiencing themselves as human beings, it would seem futile to expect that Christians as Christians would be concerned about the secular community in its gross practices of prejudice and discrimination. If a black Christian and a white Christian, in encounter, cannot reach out to each other in mutual realization because of that which they are experiencing in common, then there should be no surprise that the Christian institution has been powerless in the presence of the color bar in society. Rather it has reflected the presence of the color bar within its own institutional life.

On the other hand, if Christians practice brotherhood among Christians, this would be one limited step in the direction of a new order among men. Think of what this would mean. Wherever one Christian met or dealt with another Christian, there would be a socially redemptive encounter. They would be like the Gulf Stream or the Japanese Current tempering and softening the climate in all directions. Indeed the Christian would be a leaven at all levels of the community and in public and private living. Of course, such a situation may lend itself to all kinds of exploitation and betrayals — but the Christian would be one of the bulwarks of integrity in human relations in an immoral society. — *The Luminous Darkness*, 105

•

> There is a balm in Gilead,
> To make the spirit whole.
> There is a balm in Gilead,
> To heal the sin-sick soul.

The peculiar genius of the Negro slave is revealed here in much of its structural splendor. The setting is the Book of Jeremiah. The prophet has come to a "Dead Sea" place in his life. Not only is he discouraged over the external events in the life of Israel, but he is also spiritually depressed and tortured. As a wounded animal he cried out, "Is there no balm in Gilead? Is no physician there?" It is not a question of fact that he is raising — it is not a question directed to any particular person for an answer. It is not addressed either to God or to Israel, but rather it is a question raised by Jeremiah's entire life. He is searching his own soul. He is stripped to the literal substance of himself, and is turned back on himself for an answer. Jeremiah is saying actually, "There must be a balm in Gilead; it cannot be that there is no balm in Gilead." The relentless winnowing of his own bitter experience has laid bare his soul to the end that he is brought face to face with the very ground and core of his own faith.

The slave caught the mood of this spiritual dilemma, and with it did an amazing thing. He straightened the question mark in Jeremiah's sentence into an exclamation point: "There *is* a balm in Gilead!" Here is a note of creative triumph.

—*Deep River,* 59–60

The significance of the religion of Jesus to people who stand with their backs against the wall has always seemed to me to be crucial. It is one emphasis which has been lacking — except where it has been a part of a very unfortunate corruption of the missionary impulse, which is, in a sense, the very heartbeat of the Christian religion. My interest in the problem has been and continues to be both personal and professional. This is the question which individuals and groups who live in our land always under the threat of profound social and psychological displacement face: Why is it that Christianity seems impotent to deal radically, and therefore effectively, with the issues of discrimination and injustice on the basis of race, religion, and national origin? Is this impotency due to a betrayal of the genius of the religion, or is it due to a basic weakness in the religion itself? The question is searching, for the dramatic demonstration of the impotency of Christianity in dealing with the issues is under-scored by its apparent inability to cope with it within its own fellowship.   — *Jesus and the Disinherited,* 7–8

•

It is not my purpose here to discuss the deep polarizations within the black community that began to emerge [during the 1960s]; however, there are two important aspects in the sub-sequent unfolding of the whole-making tendency operative in Negro life. First, there was the emergence of other heroes. The psychological condition for testing the hero had been set forth in the dynamics of the social experience of the race. One of the characteristics of the awakening that followed the emergence of Martin Luther King was a search for other heroes whose magic would make room for the vital and fundamental place of aggression, that deep drive in life so central to the life of the species. It is not merely protective, shielding to life, but it also has a prowling quality that can scarcely be distinguished from belligerence. In the light of this need, the drive could not be ig-nored — it had to be utilized, if not on behalf of community, then it was mandatory that a different concept of community must be created. Just as nonviolence had become the watch-word of community in the first instance, violence became the watchword of the new concept.

What emerged as the new concept of community? The ten-dency toward whole-making was at once self-defeating if it did not establish clear-cut and fixed boundaries. Without such boundaries freedom itself had no significance, so the reason-ing ran. Therefore, it was only within fixed boundaries, *self-determined* — and that is the key word — that the goals of community could be experienced, achieved, or realized. The natural lines along which the boundaries should be set would be to separate those who had been historically victimized by so-ciety from those who had victimized them. The bankruptcy of

trust stood fully revealed. What had been whispered for so long
behind closed doors about the real relation between black and
white was now shouted in the streets and in the public forums,
followed by the demand for radical separation between black
and white. There was the strident insistence that any notion of
inclusiveness was merest illusion, and the term "brainwashed"
was applied to anyone with a contrary point of view. Such a
separation was distinguished from segregation because it was
voluntary and deliberate. Psychologically, it would utilize aggression in a manner positive and creative rather than positive
and destructive. The way was clear now for the emergence of a
new kind of hero, one who would be a new symbol — a profoundly angry man, hard and unyielding. Black now took on a
new meaning and the term "Black Power" became a fresh rallying point for a sagging self-estimate. Nothing must be as it was
before in school, church, marketplace, and territory. The winds
blew sharp and fierce across the regions of American life.

This kind of self-estimate sent the believers back into the
past, as far as human records extended. Africa became symbolic of the ideal, an ancient, yet historical expression of the
new center for the integration of the human spirit. Many rituals
appeared in varied forms — new styles of dress, of hair groom-
ing and new forms of old culinary delights. Fresh words also
entered the vocabulary — soul food, dashikis, and the Afro Hair
dress, etc. In fine, the new sense of community made for the rejection *of* the white community rather than being rejected *by*
the white community. A cause was made out of the latter rejection and a new offensive was born. The heroes were men and
women who became at once the voices of that rejection. They
were local, national, and international. The dream of a new sovereignty within the larger sovereignty became apparent. A new
political structure within the larger political superstructure put
in its challenging appearance....

Often those who stood for the old sense of community and continued to work on its behalf were regarded as "Uncle Toms." The man who was concerned about such things as good will and love beyond the new community was seen increasingly as a "traitor" to the new order. "Black is beautiful" became not merely a phrase — it was a stance, a total attitude, a metaphysic. In very positive and exciting terms it began undermining the idea that had developed over so many years into a central aspect of white mythology: that black is ugly, black is evil, black is demonic; therefore black people are ugly, evil, and demonic. In so doing it fundamentally attacked the front line of defense of the myth of white supremacy and superiority. The point at which to start would be with the children. Thus there would be a penetration into the seedbed where ideas are planted, nurtured, and developed. There began to appear new centers for black children that were not much concerned about the traditional tools of learning — reading, writing, and arithmetic — as they were about uprooting and replanting. That is fundamental....

It is not amiss to be reminded that there may be many areas of life within the black community that are disturbed at the turn of events. Perhaps the sharpest criticism is the seeming ignorance of the champions for self-determined separateness concerning the struggles of the past. The paradox is as cruel as it is apparent. On the one hand there is the insistence of reinterpretation of, and at the same time, a rejection of past history. This evident lack of a sense of history is a most damaging criticism. There seems to be no recognition of the relentless logic tying present events and ideas with what has preceded them and from which they can never be separated. The cavalier manner in which this seems to be ignored is seen as being the merest stupidity and ignorance. There is general alarm over the way in which the aggression turns on itself, inflicting havoc and wreckage on Negroes themselves. There are many who have lived deep in the heart of American society and know with certainty that to undertake to build community as a closed entity within the large society is not only suicidal but the sheerest stupidity, because it plays directly into the hands of those persons and elements in society who have stood as defenders against any and all inclusiveness as the true (American) basis of community. What they were unable to accomplish after three hundred years is now being done for them without their having to lift a finger. They are willing to encourage, to support with their money and their power all moves toward separating black from white. At last, their message has gotten through to Negroes and is being implemented by them in a manner not to be envisioned by the wildest flight of the imagination. . . .

It is my considered judgment that the present solution is a stop-gap, a halt in the line of march toward full community or, at most, a time of bivouac on a promontory overlooking the entire landscape of American society. It is time for assessing and reassessing resources in the light of the most ancient memory of the race concerning community, to hear again the clear voice of prophet and seer calling for harmony among all the children of men. At length there will begin to be talk of plans for the new city — that has never before existed on land or sea. At the center of the common life there will be strange and vaguely familiar stirrings. Some there will be whose dreams will be haunted by forgotten events in which in a moment of insight they saw a vision of a way of life transcending all barriers alien to community. Among the elder statesmen will be those through whose blood the liquid fires of Martin Luther King's dream swept all before it in one grand surge of beatific glory. They will remember and wonder at what they see about them. It will be discovered, how long and under what circumstance will remain among the mysteries, that the barriers of community can never be arbitrarily established, however necessitous it may be to seek to do so for good and saving reasons. Here and there will be those who will walk out under the stars and think

lonely thoughts about whence they came and the meaning that
their presence in the heavens inspires. They will wonder and
ponder heavy thoughts about man and his destiny under the
stars. One day there will stand up in their midst one who will
tell of a new sickness among the children who in their delirium
cry for their brothers whom they have never known and from
whom they have been cut off behind the self-imposed barriers of
their fathers. An alarm will spread throughout the community
that it is being felt and slowly realized that community cannot
feed for long on itself; it can only flourish where always the
boundaries are giving way to the coming of others from beyond
them — unknown and undiscovered brothers. Then the wisest
among them will say: What we have sought we have found,
our own sense of identity. We have an established center out
of which at last we can function and relate to other men. We
have committed to heart and to nervous system a feeling of belonging and our spirits are no longer isolated and afraid. We
have lost our fear of our brothers and are no longer ashamed
of ourselves, of who and what we are — Let us now go forth
to save the land of our birth from the plague that first drove
us into the "will to quarantine" and to separate ourselves behind self-imposed walls. For this is why we were born: Men,
all men belong to each other, and he who shuts himself away
diminishes himself, and he who shuts another away from him
destroys himself. And all the people said *Amen.*

> — *The Search for Common Ground,*
> 96–97, 97–98, 101–2, 103–4

JESUS AND THE LOVE-ETHIC

The solution which Jesus found for himself and for Israel, as
they faced the hostility of the Greco-Roman world, becomes the
word and the work of redemption for all the cast-down people

in every generation and in every age. I mean this quite literally.
I do not ignore the theological and metaphysical interpretation
of the Christian doctrine of salvation. But the underprivileged
everywhere have long since abandoned any hope that this type
of salvation deals with the crucial issues by which their days
are turned into despair without consolation. The basic fact is
that Christianity as it was born in the mind of this Jewish
teacher and thinker appears as a technique of survival for the
oppressed. That it became, through the intervening years, a religion of the powerful and the dominant, used sometimes as
an instrument of oppression, must not tempt us into believing
that it was thus in the mind and life of Jesus. "In him was life,
and the life was the light of men." Wherever his spirit appears,
the oppressed gather fresh courage; for he announced the good
news that fear, hypocrisy, and hatred, the three hounds of hell
that track the trail of the disinherited, need have no dominion
over them.   — *Jesus and the Disinherited,* 28–29

Living in a climate of deep insecurity, Jesus, faced with so nar-
row a margin of civil guarantees, had to find some other basis
upon which to establish a sense of well-being. He knew that the
goals of religion as he understood them could never be worked
out within the then-established order. Deep from within that
order he projected a dream, the logic of which would give to
all the needful security. There would be room for all, and no
man would be a threat to his brother. "The kingdom of God is
within." "The Spirit of the Lord is upon me, because he hath
anointed me to preach the gospel to the poor."

The basic principles of his way of life cut straight through
to the despair of his fellows and found it groundless. By infer-
ence he says, "You must abandon your fear of each other and
fear only God. You must not indulge in any deception and dis-
honesty, even to save your lives. Your words must be Yea —
Nay; anything else is evil. Hatred is destructive to hated and

hater alike. Love your enemy, that you may be children of your Father who is in heaven." — *Jesus and the Disinherited*, 34–35

The central emphasis of the teaching of Jesus centers upon the relationship of individual to individual, and of all individuals to God. So profound has been the conviction of Christians as to the ultimate significance of his teaching about love that they have rested their case, both for the validity and the supremacy of the Christian religion, at this point. When someone asked Jesus what is the meaning of all the law and the prophets, he gave those tremendous words of Judaism, "Hear, O Israel, the Lord thy God is One, and thou shalt love the Lord thy God with all thy mind, heart, soul and strength. Thou shalt love thy neighbor as thyself." Jesus rests his case for the ultimate significance of life on the love ethic. Love is the intelligent, kindly but stern expression of kinship of one individual for another, having as its purpose the maintenance and furtherance of life at its highest level. Self-love is the kind of activity having as its purpose the maintenance and furtherance of one's own life at its highest level. All love grows basically out of a qualitative self-regard and is in essence the exercise of that which is spiritual. If we accept the basic proposition that all life is one, arising out of a common center — God, all expressions of love are acts of God. Hate, then, becomes a form of annihilation of self and others; in short — suicide.   — *Deep Is the Hunger*, 108–9

The religion of Jesus says to the disinherited: "Love your enemy. Take the initiative in seeking ways by which you can have the experience of a common sharing of mutual worth and value. It may be hazardous, but you must do it." For the Negro it means that he must see the individual white man in the context of a common humanity. The fact that a particular individual is white, and therefore may be regarded in some over-all sense as

the racial enemy, must be faced; and opportunity must be provided, found, or created for freeing such an individual from his
"white necessity." From this point on, the relationship becomes
like any other primary one.

Once an attack is made on the enemy status and the individual has emerged, the underprivileged man must himself be
status free. It may be argued that his sense of freedom must
come first. Here I think the answer may be determined by the
one who initiates the activity. But in either case love is possible
only between two freed spirits. What one discovers in even a
single experience in which barriers have been removed may become useful in building an over-all technique for loving one's
enemy. There cannot be too great insistence on the point that
we are here dealing with a discipline, a method, a technique, as
over against some form of wishful thinking or simple desiring.

—*Jesus and the Disinherited*, 100–101

•

The crucifixion of Jesus Christ reminds us once again of the
penalty which any highly organized society exacts of those
who violate its laws. The social resistors fall into two general
groups — those who resist the established order by doing the
things that are in opposition to accepted standards of decency
and morality: the criminal, the antisocial, the outlaw; and those
who resist the established order because its requirements are too
low, too unworthy of the highest and best in man. Each is a
menace to organized society and both must be liquidated as dis-
turbers of the peace. Behold then the hill outside of the city of
Jerusalem, the criminal and the Holy Man sharing a common
judgment, because one rose as high above the conventions of
his age as the other descended below. Perhaps it is ever thus.
Whenever a Jesus Christ is crucified, there will also be crucified
beside him the thief — two symbols of resistance to the established pattern. When Christianity makes central in its doctrine

the redemptive significance of the cross, it defines itself ever in terms of the growing edge, the advance guard of the human race, who take the lead in man's long march to the City of God.

— *Deep Is the Hunger*, 31

NONVIOLENCE AND RECONCILING COMMUNITY

"No one ever wins a fight" — thoughtfully, and with eyes searching the depths of me, my grandmother repeated the words. I was something to behold. One eye was swollen, my jacket was ripped with all the buttons torn from their places, and there was a large tear in the right knee of my trousers. It was a hard and bitter fight. I had stood all I could, until at last I threw discretion to the winds and the fight was on. The fact that he was larger and older and had brothers did not matter. For four blocks we had fought and there was none to separate us. At last I began to gain in power; with one tremendous effort I got him to the ground and, as the saying went, "made him eat dirt." Then I had come home to face my grandmother. "No one ever wins a fight," were her only words as she looked at me. "But I beat him," I said. "Yes, but look at you. You beat him, but you will learn someday that nobody ever wins a fight." Many years have come and gone since that afternoon in early summer. I have seen many fights, big and little. I have lived through two world wars. The wisdom of these telling words becomes clearer as the days unfold. There is something seductive about the quickening sense of power that comes when the fight is on. There is a bewitching something men call honor, in behalf of which they often do and become the dishonorable thing. It is all very strange. How often honor is sacrificed in defense of honor. Honor is often a strange mixture of many things — pride, fear, hate, shame, courage, truth, cowardice —

many things. The mind takes many curious twistings and turn-
ings as it runs the interference for one's survival. And yet the
term survival alone is not quite what is meant. Men want to survive, yes, but on their own terms. And this is most often what is
meant by honor. "No one ever wins a fight." This suggests that
there is always some other way; or does it mean that man can
always choose the weapons he shall use? Not to fight at all is
to choose a weapon by which one fights. Perhaps the authentic
moral stature of a man is determined by his choice of weapons
which he uses in his fight against the adversary. Of all weapons,
love is the most deadly and devastating, and few there be who
dare trust their fate in its hands.

—*Deep Is the Hunger*, 10–11

The Moment of Recollection

In Thy presence, our Father, we make an act of recollection:

We cradle in tenderness those that have been visited by
sudden or muted violences; families shattered by death and
murder; those distraught by illness which does not respond to
the trained mind and the skilled hand; those who inhabit the
shadows where things are never clear to the mind and at the
core of whose spirit lies an endless torture, making for restlessness, panic, and madness; children who are without love and
compassion, who must manage life with ill-formed and blunted
tools; the lonely who cannot experience the penetration of the
wall that envelops them; and those who are so tired that the
ground of their being is consumed by a great weariness. These
we remember before Thee, our Father.

We do not know how to express our feelings, we do not
know quite what to say. We give to Thee a cloud of witnesses to
human need that in Thee may be found sanctuary for them. As
for us, we still ourselves in Thy presence to be caught up by the
movement of Thy spirit in our minds and hearts so that we may

dare become Thy living agents of usefulness and redemption. Grant, O gracious God, that we may not betray Thy urgency through self-love, self-pity, or fear. This our souls cannot abide. Deliver us from so great a temptation, our Father.

— *The Centering Moment*, 42

The Experience of Love

There is a steady anxiety that surrounds man's experience of love. Sometimes the radiance of love is so soft and gentle that the individual sees himself with all harsh lines wiped away and all limitations blended with his strengths in so happy a combination that strength seems to be everywhere and weakness is nowhere to be found. This is a part of the magic, the spell of love. Sometimes the radiance of love kindles old fires that have long since grown cold from the neglect of despair, or new fires are kindled by a hope born full-blown without beginning and without ending. Sometimes the radiance of love blesses a life with a vision of its possibilities never before dreamed of or sought, stimulating new endeavor and summoning all latent powers to energize the life at its inmost core.

But there are other ways by which love works its perfect work. It may stab the spirit by calling forth a bitter, scathing self-judgment. The heights to which it calls may seem so high that all incentive is lost and the individual is stricken with an utter hopelessness and despair. It may throw in relief old and forgotten weaknesses to which one has made the adjustment of acceptance — but which now stir in their place to offer themselves as testimony of one's unworthiness and to challenge the love with their embarrassing authenticity. It is at such times that one expects love to be dimmed under the mistaken notion that love is at long last based upon merit and worth.

Behold the miracle! Love has no awareness of merit or demerit; it has no scale by which its portion may be weighed or measured. It does not seek to balance giving and receiving. Love loves; this is its nature. But this does not mean that love is blind, naïve, or pretentious. It does mean that love holds its object securely in its grasp, calling all that it sees by its true name but surrounding all with a wisdom born both of its passion and its understanding. Here is no traffic in sentimentality, no catering to weakness or to strength. Instead, there is robust vitality that quickens the roots of personality, creating an unfolding of the self that redefines, reshapes, and makes all things new. Such an experience is so fundamental in quality that an individual knows that what is happening to him can outlast all things without itself being dissipated or lost.

Whence comes this power which seems to be the point of referral for all experience and the essence of all meaning? No created thing, no single unit of life, can be the source of such fullness and completeness. For in the experience itself a man is caught and held by something so much more than he can ever think or be that there is but one word by which its meaning can be encompassed — God. Hence the Psalmist says that as long as the love of God shines on us undimmed, not only may no darkness obscure but also we may find our way to a point in other hearts beyond all weakness and all strength, beyond all that is good and beyond all that is evil. There is no thing outside ourselves, no circumstance, no condition, no vicissitude, that can ultimately separate us from the love of God and from the love of one another. And we pour out our gratitude to God that this is so!   — *The Inward Journey,* 35–36

•

Thus nonviolence occurs and recurs on the horizon throughout man's life. It is one of the great vehicles of reconciliation because it creates and maintains a climate in which the need to be cared for and understood can be honored and effectively dealt with. The mood of nonviolence is that of reconciliation.

It engenders in the individual an attitude that inspires wholeness and integration within. It provides the climate in which the things that are needed for peace, or for one's own peace, may be sensed, disclosed, and developed. It presupposes that the desire to be cared for and to care for others is one with the very essence of all one's meaning and significance. It thus provides a working atmosphere in which this mutual desiring may be normal, reasonable, and accepted.

But nonviolence is not merely a mood or climate, or even an attitude. It is a technique and, in and of itself, a discipline. In the first place, it is a rejection of physical force, a renunciation of the tools of physical violence. These may be renounced because they are not available; such a renunciation has only tactical significance. Here nonviolence may be used effectively by violent men as a practical necessity. In this sense it has the same moral basis as violence. This is one of the ancient weapons of the weak against the strong and is a part of the over-all tactic of deception. It is instructive to note that when nonviolence is used in this way in response to external necessity, this may not at all vitiate its creative impact upon those against whom it is used. The importance of this cannot be overemphasized. Because nonviolence is an affirmation of the *existence* of the man of violent deeds, in contradistinction to the fact that violence embodies a will to *nonexistence,* the moral impact which nonviolence carries may potentially realize itself in a given situation by rendering the violent act ineffective and bringing about the profoundest kind of change in attitude. All this may take place in encounter, even though the users of nonviolence are full of violence themselves. This is apt to be true in situations where the tools for physical violence are not available, or because even if used, the chances for their success are poor. It is entirely possible for an individual to use nonviolence with detachment — as an effective weapon and a substitute for weapons of violence —

while the mood continues to be violent, a mood that inspires hate, that wills the nonexistence of another. . . .

But the psychological tools of nonviolence are of another order. Their purpose is to open the door of the heart so that what another is feeling and experiencing can find its way within. They assume that it is possible for a man to get real insight into the meaning of his deeds, attitudes, or way of life as they affect the life of his fellows. A man faced with nonviolence is forced to deal with himself, finally; every way of escape is ultimately cut off. This is why there can be no possible limit as to time or duration of nonviolent acts. Their purpose is not merely to change an odious situation, but, further, to make it urgent for a man to face himself in his action. Finally all must face the same basic question: Is what I am doing an expression of my fundamental intent toward any man when I am most myself? The more persistent nonviolent acts become, the more threatening they are to the person who refuses to deal with the ultimate question. . . .

When there is a face-to-face encounter between nonviolence as a tool in the hands of a nonviolent man and violence as a tool in the hands of a violent man, the human element makes reconciliation a real potential in the situation. Unless the actual status of a human being as such is denied, reconciliation between people always has a chance to be effective. But when this status is denied, a major reappraisal or reassessment must take place *before* the work of reconciliation — which is the logic of nonviolence — can become effective. . . .

The purpose of his use of nonviolence as a collective device is to awaken conscience and an awareness of the evil of a violent system, and to make available the experience of the collective destiny in which all people in the system are participating. There is always the possibility that the effect of the nonviolent technique will be to solidify and organize the methods of violence used in counteraction. There is nothing unnatural here.

Clearly, if the system is altered along the lines of the needs of those who are practicing nonviolence, then a profound change has to take place within the power structure so that *all* may share the fruits of the common life. The resistance to nonviolence discussed here is the last line of defense of those who cannot yet understand or feel that the ancient need to be cared for and understood, and to care for and understand, is asserting itself. And this is, at last, the work of reconciliation. The discipline for all who are involved has the same aim — to find a way to honor what is deepest in one person and to have that person honor what is deepest in the other.

> — *Disciplines of the Spirit*, 114–15,
> 115–16, 119, 120–21

There is a spirit abroad in life of which the Judaeo-Christian ethic is but one expression. It is a spirit that makes for wholeness and for community; it finds its way into the quiet solitude of a Supreme Court justice when he ponders the constitutionality of an act of Congress which guarantees civil rights to all its citizens; it settles in the pools of light in the face of a little girl as with her frailty she challenges the hard frightened heart of a police chief; it walks along the lonely road with the solitary protest marcher and settles over him with a benediction as he falls by the assassin's bullet fired from ambush; it kindles the fires of unity in the heart of Jewish Rabbi, Catholic Priest, and Protestant Minister as they join arms together, giving witness to their God on behalf of a brotherhood that transcends creed, race, sex, and religion; it makes a path to Walden Pond and ignites the flame of nonviolence in the mind of a Thoreau and burns through his liquid words from the Atlantic to the Pacific; it broods over the demonstrators for justice and brings comfort to the desolate and forgotten who have no memory of what it is to feel the rhythm of belonging to the race of men; it knows no country and its allies are to be found wherever the heart is kind and the collective will and the private endeavor seek to make justice where injustice abounds, to make peace where chaos is rampant, and to make the voice heard on behalf of the helpless and the weak. It is the voice of God and the voice of man; it is the meaning of all the strivings of the whole human race toward a world of friendly men underneath a friendly sky.

— *The Luminous Darkness,* 112–13

Chapter 3

The Authentic Self

Howard Thurman believes that beneath the many identities we wear — whether those bestowed by family, friends, or culture — there is in each of us a core identity given by God. This identity is one's true self. This self is of ultimate worth; it cannot be diminished by the assessments of others. One's own failures may be tragic, but the value of the self remains. It can be betrayed, ignored, abused, or forgotten; still, its God-given worth remains constant.

A sense of self is an essential aspect of all religious experience. A self encounters God. A self comes to know security in God. A self gains new confidence for engaging life. A self commits to the spiritual disciplines. A self mediates the meaning of religious experience for the individual and for community. The self is God's instrument of relationship and service. The failure to have a true sense of self impairs responsiveness to God. Vigilance in awareness and care of one's self is therefore a spiritual concern of the first order.

But one's availability to God is compromised if the self is absorbed in serving other gods. The gods of materialism, prestige, power, self-pity, and anxiety all demand full allegiance. They promise a complete identity and feelings of fulfillment, but they are incapable of delivering these for the full stretch of life. Their primary purpose is not to fulfill the self, but to enslave it. Thurman stresses that the true self's freedom comes only through surrender to God. To refuse this surrender is to be adrift in life — going nowhere.

God created us for relationship with God and God's creation. Thurman believes the relational self fulfills its deepest hunger when it seeks to experience God's holiness in all things. The encounters with God's holiness provide joy and "the peace which surpasses all understanding." The self's challenge is to be sensitive and responsive to the opportunities for such encounters. Thurman asserts that living the spiritually disciplined life enables each person to be "alive to life." For Thurman, one must be attentive to holy encounters and revelations that occur in the most ordinary of places and events, as well as in those designated as sacred places and events. His meditations are often about ultimate meanings that surface from mundane situations. Community is the place where the self is forever discovering opportunities for holy encounters and therefore opportunities for fulfillment.

At the same time, anyone who is alive to life will come to know the pervasiveness of death. Every expression of life is temporal, and so the self must make sense of death. But if the self cannot eliminate death, it can eliminate its fear *of death. Here again, Thurman stresses how the spiritual disciplines prepare one to address the onslaught of trouble that come with life. Loved ones die. Wars ravage the land. Dreams are deferred. Hopes are crushed. Suffering kills the innocent. Still, the self is capable of living through devastating experiences and then persevering with newfound strength and joy. Through ongoing encounters with God and renewal of the self, the fear of death can be overcome. Experiences of coming alive again after exhaustion, trauma, and defeat reassure the self of God's renewing and eternal love and power. For the journey, this reassurance is enough.*

CENTERED IN GOD

My testimony is that life is against all dualism. Life is One. Therefore, a way of life that is worth living must be a way worthy of life itself. Nothing less than that can abide. Always, against all that fragments and shatters and against all things that separate and divide within and without, life labors to meld together into a single harmony.

Therefore, failure may remain failure in the context of all our strivings, hatred may continue to be hatred in the social and political arena of the common life, tragedy may continue to yield its anguish and its pain, spreading havoc in the tight circle of our private lives, the dead weight of guilt may not shift its position to make life even for a brief moment more comfortable and endurable, for any of us — all this may be true. Nevertheless, in all these things there is a secret door which leads into the central place, where the Creator of life and the God of the human heart are one and the same. I take my stand for the future and for the generations who follow over the bridges we already have crossed. It is here that the meaning of the hunger of the heart is unified. The Head and the Heart at last inseparable; they are lost in wonder in the One.   — *With Head and Heart*, 269

It may seem to be splitting hairs to say that Destiny is what a man does with his fate. Fate is given; Destiny is won. Fate is the raw materials of experience. They come uninvited and often unanticipated. Destiny is what a man does with these raw materials. A man participates in his fate almost as a spectator or perhaps as a victim; he does not call the tunes. It is important to make clear that this is only an aspect of human experience. To ignore the margin of experience that seems to be unresponsive to any private will or desire is disastrous. To ascribe responsibility for all the things that happen to one to some kind of fate is equally disastrous. It is quite reasonable to say that there are

forces in life that are set in motion by something beyond the
power of man to comprehend or control. The purpose of such
forces, their significance, what it is that they finally mean for
human life, only God knows. The point at which they touch us
or affect us cannot be fully understood. Why they affect us as
they do, what they mean in themselves, we do not know. Sometimes they seem like trial and error, like accidents, like blind
erratic power that is without conscience or consciousness, only
a gross aliveness. To say that those forces are evil or good presupposes a knowledge of ends which we do not have. The point
at which they affect our lives determines whether we call them
good or evil. This is a private judgment that we pass upon a
segment of our primary contact with the forces of life. Out of
this contact we build our destiny. We determine what we shall
do with our circumstances. It is here that religion makes one
of its most important contributions to life. It is a resource that
provides strength, stability and confidence as one works at one's
destiny. It gives assurance of a God who shares in the issue and
whose everlasting arms are always there.

> I know not where His islands lift
> Their fronded palms in air.
> I only know I cannot drift
> Beyond his love and care.

— *Deep Is the Hunger,* 42–43

•

The insight of the spiritual ["Jacob's Ladder"] is not only confined to the gothic principle and this sense of tomorrow, which
are truly kindred notions, but there is implicit here that each
man must face the figure at the top of the ladder. There is a
goal. It is some kind of climax to human history. Every man
must come to terms with the ultimate problem. How does he

relate to something that is final in existence? In one way or another God and the human spirit must come together. Whatever things in life you believe to be true and valid, you and they must sit together in the solitude of your own spirit; and when you do what is on the agenda no form of pretension has any standing there. Even your most vaunting ambition may seem in such a moment to be filthy rags. The one searching item with which you have to deal is, how have you lived your life in the knowledge of your truth? This may not occur for the individual at the time of his dying, or at a moment of crisis, but as you turn the corner today in your own road, suddenly it is upon you. We are all climbing Jacob's ladder, and every round goes higher and higher. All who recognize this as a living part of their experience join with those early destiny-bound singers who marched through all the miseries of slavery confident that they could never be entirely earth-bound.   — *Deep River,* 86–87

The Many Selves Become One

In Thy Presence we become aware of many divisions within the inner circle of the Self. When we enter into communion with Thee, we are never sure of the Voice that speaks within us. We do not always know which voice is the true Voice.

Sometimes it is the clear call of the heart remembering an unfulfilled hunger from other days; sometimes it is but an echo of some "failing impulse to good" which we have pushed aside that a private end may triumph even in the face of the distinct call of truth; often it is the muttering of needs that do not shape themselves in words because they are one with all the ebb and flow of every passing day; at times the Voice is like a clarion rising above all conflicts and confusion, so uttering the need for courage to stand against some evil, to witness for the good where the cost is high and the penalty great; sometimes the Voice is muted, telling of hopes unrealized and dreams that will not rest until they incarnate themselves in us — all the while we pull back but they will not let us go.

In the midst of all the sounds rising above all the mingled words there is a strange Voice — but not quite a stranger. A man recognizes it. It seems to come from every part of him but cannot rest itself on any point of sound. He waits. He listens. When all is still, he listens now at a deeper level of silence. In soundless movement there floats up through all the chambers of his being, encompassing all the tongued cries from many selves, one word: God — God — God. And the answer is the same, filling all the living silence before Thy Face: God — God — God.
— *The Inward Journey,* 135–36

When I Awake, I Am Still with Thee
[Psalm 139:18]

In all the waking hours
The Tentacles of Time
Give channel to each living thing:
 The bird on wing;
 The mole moving in darkness underground;
 The cricket chanting its evening song;
 The primeval whale sporting in chilly seas,
  or floating noiselessly in turbulent waters;
In mountain crevice or sprawling meadow
The delicate beauty of color-stained flower
 or fragile leaf;
High above the timber line
 The sprig of green dares wind and snow;
In the barren parchness of desert waste
 The juiceless shrub and waterlogged cactus;
High in the treetop the green-pearled fruit
 of olive mistletoe,
  and the soft gray stillness of creeping moss;

The infant, the growing child,
The stumbling adolescent, the young adult,
The man full blown or stooped with years;
The Tentacles of Time
Give channel to each living thing.

And beyond this?
Thoughts that move with grace of being:
Light thoughts that dance and sing
Untouched by gloom or shadow or the dark;
Weighty thoughts that press upon the road
with tracks that blossom into dreams
or shape themselves in plan and scheme;
Thoughts that whisper;
Thoughts that shout;
Thoughts that wander without rest,
Seeking, seeking, always seeking;
Thoughts that challenge;
Thoughts that soothe;
The Tentacles of Time
Give Channel to each living thing.

Out from the House of Life
All things come,
And into it, each returns again for rest.

When I awake,
I am still with Thee.

— The Inward Journey, 151–52

The Sustainer of Life

It is of enormous reassurance to us, our Father, that Thou art
the sustainer and the holder of life, that despite all of our own

limitations and finitudes, despite all our weaknesses and failures, despite all of the soarings of our minds and imaginations
and our spirits, always we come back to the deeply-lying assurance that Thou art the sustainer of life, the holder of all
creation, and the guarantor of all our values. This is of such
overwhelming reassurance to us that we celebrate in simple
words of praise this almighty grace.

We offer on our part not merely the good deeds of which
we are aware at times, not merely the concerns for our fellows
which sometimes lead us to simple deeds or glorious acts of self-
sacrifice, but we offer Thee the things that we might become —
all of the possibilities of our lives, the potentials not yet realized.
We offer to Thee our failures also; those times when something
breaks down and we do not know what, or when something
breaks down and we do know what; all that we might have been
at a particular time and were not; all of the sense of conscience
that disturbs and whips and tortures because we have not been
in quality and in kind what we knew at the time we could have
been in quality and kind. And beyond all of these expressions of
ourselves, our Father, we offer to Thee ourselves. This is what
we want to do, and sometimes we are able to do it — just to
say to Thee, Father, here am I. My life as it is at its depth I
give to Thee. And I want Thee to hold it so that it is no longer
my life to do with in accordance with my whims, my impulses,
my desires, or even my needs, but to take my life and to hold
it until it takes on Thy character, Thy mind, Thy purposes. If
Thou wilt do this and if Thou wilt help me to do this, then I can
be in myself what is truest and surest in me. And this, O God, is
all, all, all.   — *The Centering Moment,* 111

The Inward Sea

There is in every person an inward sea, and in that sea there
is an island and on that island there is an altar and standing

guard before that altar is the "angel with the flaming sword." Nothing can get by that angel to be placed upon that altar unless it has the mark of your inner authority. Nothing passes "the angel with the flaming sword" to be placed upon your altar unless it be a part of "the fluid area of your consent." This is your crucial link with the Eternal.   — *Meditations of the Heart*, 15

THE MEANING OF SELF

We turn now to explore the meaning of commitment more directly in terms of personality. There are three questions an individual must ask himself, and in his answers he will find the meaning of commitment for himself: Who am I? What do I want? How do I propose to get it?

Let us take these in order. Who am I? It is a commonplace that each of us seems to have many selves. Of the numerous encounters the Master had with individuals, none is more dramatic than his meeting with a certain madman, who stood staring at Him out of eyes that reflected the agonizing turmoil within. From his wrists dangled broken chains. He was regarded by his community as possessed by devils; there were times when he became so violent that, as a measure of collective defense, he was seized and chained to rocks. Even then he could not be restrained when the turbulence within him leaped into muscle, bone, and sinew. The chains burst with the pressure and he would go shrieking through the waste places like a wounded animal. This was the creature who faced the Master. He cried out to be let alone. And with gentleness, tenderness, and vast compassion, soft words issued from the mouth of Jesus: "What is your name? Who are you?" And the whole dam broke, and he cried, "My name is Legion!" He might have said: "This is the pit of my agony. There are so many of me, and they riot in my street. If only I could know who I am — which one is me —

then I would be whole again. I would have a center, a self, a rallying point deep within me for all the chaos, until at last the chaos would become order."

Fundamental, then, to any experience of commitment is the yielding of the *real* citadel. It must be said again that the process may be slow and devious. Within us all are so many claims and counterclaims that to honor the true self is not easy.

— *Disciplines of the Spirit*, 26–27

The quest for stability is pursued against a background of threatening confusion and impelled by a desire for personal morale. Its achievement results in a profound *sense of self*. It is important, therefore, to find out what a *sense of self* may mean as the object of our search. In the first place, one's personal stability depends on his relationships with others. For, in order to answer the question, "Who am I?" the individual must go on to ask, "To whom, to what do I belong?" This primary sense of belonging, of counting, of participating in situations, of sharing with the group, is the basis of all personal stability. And from it is derived the true *sense of self*. We are all related either positively or negatively to some immediate social unit which provides the other-than-self reference which in turn undergirds the sense of self. Such a primary group confers *persona* upon the individual; it fashions and fortifies the character structure. It is so important that most of our choices, decisions and actions are taken in the light of their bearing upon our relationship with the group or groups that give to us dignity, self-respect, status, a sense of self. Whenever I ask myself, "What do I wish — what do I want to do?" I am almost sure to raise the broader question, "How will this affect my standing with others?" For experience tells us that disapproval and criticisms are likely to emasculate or even to annihilate our sense of self and so to strip us of all personal significance. At such moments, if we can find a strong personality to lean to, we fasten upon him with such utter dependence that we become in important ways his reflection. Sometimes, after a bitter humiliation, when we so greatly need help for our healing, for being made whole again, we are introduced to a personality who brings us what we need and stays with us, until slowly, and often with great pain, we are able to stand on our own feet once more. And so we regain personal stability. Another question that we instinctively ask is, "What am I?" The answer rests in part with the quality of our achievements — our ability to express ourselves in effective action. Yet no one's deeds offer an adequate account of his entire personality. There is always a margin of self not quite involved in whatever he may be thinking, saying or doing at any particular moment. For each person is both a *participant* and a *spectator*. No self-expression can be perfectly complete.

— *Deep Is the Hunger,* 63–64

•

What is it we want, really? When we try to meet it head on we discover, perhaps for the first time, that we have never lived our lives intentionally, and therefore now are unable to do it on demand. When a man faces this question put to him by life, or when he is caught up in the necessity of answering it, or by deliberate intent seeks an answer, he is at once involved in the dynamics of commitment. At such a moment he knows what, in the living of his life, he must be *for* and what he must be *against*.

Finally comes the question: How do I propose to get what I want? Here is involved the whole notion of means, of procedures. All the perils of the preoccupation with self and its fulfillment enter belligerently into the arena to do battle. The more clearly I see my direction, the more discriminating I am able to be about the means of following it. If I feel that time is running out, or that what I need for my journey is threatened by others because of their blindness, selfishness, or greed, then

I may find it quite in order to be ruthless in seizing from their stubborn hands what I must have. If they will not give in, then I will take it even if it means destroying them in the process. If this is my outlook, the only morality that binds me is the need to secure that without which my own life is diminished, if not destroyed. If my commitment — which grows out of my answer to the question "What do I want?" — is for me the most important thing in the world, as indeed it may be, I may say to myself: Woe to any man who stands in my way!

If the commitment in itself becomes more important than what I am committed to — or, in other words, if the means become more important than the end — then I am prepared to be quite blind to other consequences. It is possible for a man to make an idol of commitment. We see this not merely in regard to political or social goals or systems such as fascism, communism, or democracy. Such blindness is conceivable even on what we think is the way to the Kingdom of God. A man may be so fierce and unswerving in his commitment to what is clearly to him the Kingdom of God in the world that he does all kinds of violence to his fellows in his pursuit of it. All the tenderness and compassion of his spirit harden, and with grim vigor in his righteous dedication he may easily become a religious bigot. Simply that and nothing more....

Indeed, the particular goal may be out of line with a man's possibilities as he sees them, but here he must proceed with great caution; it is possible that what he is committed to may seem, in terms of its empirical implications, so remote in the time of its fulfillment that he will decide he was mistaken. The religious experience of the individual is most important at this point. If, out of a man's fundamental commitment to God, he is led to work on behalf of a fulfillment so high that its full realization is not even in sight, then he must interpret his share as that of participating in a collective destiny as far removed from the present as the divine event itself. Instead of looking forward to a rounded fulfillment or achievement of his goal, he knows that his role is but a part of a larger whole.

— *Disciplines of the Spirit*, 34–35, 36

•

Is this a world with moral meaning at the center? This is the primary question. It must be answered before other questions can even be asked. True, it can never be answered with proof and finality, but some answer must be given on the level of faith. In history, men have often tried to side-step facing the question by saying, "We can never know"; but it cannot be side-stepped. To decide not to decide, is to decide against. The negation of inactivity is just as potent as the emphatic vocal "No!" Only when one has said "Yes," or has said "No," or has given what amounts to "No" by saying nothing — only then can one face the other basic problems: since there is meaning, what is the nature of that meaning? or since there is no meaning, how shall we act in accordance with this terrible negative? Life affirmation is not possible unless we summon enough courage to make the first basic act of faith: "I believe that there is moral meaning at the center of life!" Unfortunately, it is easily possible — much too easily possible — to make this affirmation with gusto and enthusiasm without really meaning it. Not that it is easy to be insincere, but that it is difficult really to mean it. This is simply because there is evidence on either side. We see the sordid and the tragic in life; we see the pain and suffering. This is evidence, we may say, against there being meaning at the center. Then we see beauty, truth, love, and fulfillment, and we say, "This is evidence on behalf of meaning." And the evidence is always straining within us. In consequence, we may decide intellectually in favor of meaning, only to find our subconscious casting a dissenting ballot. Douglas Steere says most of us are not integrated selves but each of us is a whole committee of selves and

decisions are made by majority vote. The result is vocal life affirmation, and active live negation. We are committed to meaning
only in an equivocal way. Therefore, the great labor of life, after
we have made the initial life affirmation, is to validate the decision in practice. After all, how can one believe that life has
meaning, if his own life does not have meaning? No words, no
matter how eloquently and enthusiastically uttered, can replace
the expressiveness of action. Indeed, words become true when
they are lived, and they become untrue when the living of them
is neglected. We shall always be ambivalent, and our "Yes" will
never have the total assent of our total wills. Our great labor
is simply to bring active affirmation as close as possible to the
vocal affirmation. All else is subsidiary.

— *Deep Is the Hunger,* 68–70

There is an order, a moral order in which men participate, that
gathers up into itself, dimensional fulfillment, limitless in its creativity and design. Whatever may be the pressures to which one
is subjected, the snares, the buffetings, one must not for a moment think that there is not an ultimate value always at stake.
It is this ultimate value at stake in all experience that is the final
incentive to decency, to courage and hope. Human life, even the
life of a slave, must be lived worthily of so grand an undertaking. At every moment a crown was placed over his head
that he must constantly grow tall enough to wear. Only of that
which is possessed of infinite potentials, can an infinite demand
be required. The unfulfilled, the underdeveloped only has a future; the fulfilled, the rounded out, the finished can only have
a past. The human spirit participates in both past and future in
what it regards as the *present* but it is independent of both.

— *The Negro Spiritual Speaks of Life and Death,* 134–35

Thus I begin with the obvious proposition that I am not alien
to life. I am a creature grounded and rooted in creatureliness.

Therefore I am a participant in the life process rather than being an isolate within it. Truly, I am a space binder; as I described earlier, my body participates completely in the life process and it is nourished and sustained by ancient processes as old as life, and set in motion before any awareness of or knowledge about them was in evidence. As a creature, I am the inheritor of age-old wisdom. Hence there can be no sense of self on the part of the individual where there is no self-conscious experience of the body as one's own unique, private, and peculiar possession. The body is a man's intimate dwelling place; it is his domain as nothing else can ever be. It is coextensive with himself. If for any reason whatsoever a man is alienated in his own body either by shame, outrage, or brutality, his sense of community within himself is rendered difficult, if not impossible. It is small wonder that one of the oldest creeds of the Christian faith carries the phrase: I believe in the resurrection of the body. For many believers the affirmation that death does not ultimately separate a man from his body makes of death a little thing.

— *The Search for Common Ground*, 78

Our Hearts Are Wooed

Again and again we find ourselves deeply distressed because there is so much that is dependent upon us as individuals carrying specific responsibilities within a world which is small and compact and demanding. So overwhelming is this kind of pressure upon us that we are tempted to rely, despite all of our inadequacies, upon our own strength. Again and again we say to ourselves, if I do not depend upon myself, if I do not depend upon that which I am able to do for myself and those for whom I am responsible, then there is no other source upon which I may be dependent. And even as we say it and as we feel it, our minds are flooded with multitudinous instances in which strength did come to us that was not of our making, a lift to our burden did come, even though it could not be measured by anything that we ourselves were doing. All around us there are these surprises of kindly interference manifesting the grace of life and the tenderness and the mercy of God.

> Thus our hearts are wooed into thanksgiving and praise for so much that has come to us, transcending our merit and our demerit, so much thoughtfulness, so much reassurance, so many little ways by which our spirits have been renewed and revived. Even against our disposition, we offer our thanksgiving to Thee. Accept it, our Father, as our sacrament and as our offering to Thee, totally, wholeheartedly, that after this hour has passed each may know for himself that he is Thy child and Thou art his Father.
>
> Our times are in Thy hand.

— The Centering Moment, 51

Our Stubborn Wills

We are deeply conscious of our stubborn wills, the hard core of resistance to Thy Spirit, as it would wisen our minds, make tender our hearts, and sensitize our spirits, our Father. We want to yield ourselves to Thee. We want to give over into Thy custody the things that disturb us, that frighten us, that fill our days with uneasiness and our nights with the kind of foreboding that challenges sleep and rest. This we want to do but we don't know how to do it. Besides, we are never sure that we can trust Thee with the things that are intimately a part of the fabric of our lives. To be rid of them would be to expose ourselves in ways that may destroy the kind of balance with which we function from day to day.

We wait now in Thy Presence with the silent hope that something may transpire within us that will relax the hold we have on the things that do not make for our peace. While we wait we remember. We remember those whose lives are a part of our own lives in ways that are direct and sure. We would include them in this waiting moment, but here again, our Father, we are not sure that this is what we really want to do. We wait, that our spirits may be clarified and our willingness may be at the disposal of the demands of our hearts. We remember our world and all the excitement of the last few days. We are troubled in our spirits because one part of us wishes so much that we may win the race for power and another part of us wishes so much that we may give ourselves freely and completely to the quest for truth on the earth, in the heavens, and in the hearts of men, and trust the decision of power to Thee in whom at last all power finally rests. With all arrogances put aside, with all weaknesses laid bare, with all our deep-lying hungers exposed, we wait, our Father, for the baptism of Thy Spirit, that we may walk confidently on the earth by the strength of our hearts and the inspiration of Thy Spirit. If this be our portion, it is enough, O God, our Father. This is enough.

— *The Centering Moment*, 70

The Meaning of Our Own Lives

Our Father, we gather ourselves together in all of our available parts to see if somehow there may be made clear for us the meaning of our own lives and the meaning of the journey to which we are committed. We confess our sins, as we wait in Thy presence, those things within us of which we are grossly ashamed, those things within us and those expressions of our lives of which we are scarcely aware until our spirits are sensitized by Thy spirit, things which do violence to Thy purposes and Thy will for us and our world. We want to be better than we are. So often we do not know how. Again and again we are moved by the impulse to be better than we are but we do not quite know how to give way to it, that it might sweep through us with its renewal and its inspiration. We are such divided, tempest-tossed, driven children. If we knew the right words to say, our Father, we would say them, if somehow we could bring our minds and our hearts into focus so that what we mean we say, and what we say we do. If we could do this, it would help us to be whole. Shall we seek to make peace within ourselves by the ordering of our wills in accordance with Thy will, or shall we seek to help those about us whose needs are great and in helping them perhaps find wholeness for ourselves? What shall we do, our Father?

Oh, that we might be unanimous within ourselves, that our total being and our lives might be a tuned instrument in Thy hands, making the kind of music that would calm the distressed, that would heal the broken body and mind, that would bring tenderness to those who feel rejected and outcast. As we wait in Thy presence, our Father, gather us in, that we might be a lung through which Thy spirit may breathe. Is this asking too much? We wait, O God our Father, we wait.

— *The Centering Moment*, 84

LIVING AS A FREE PERSON

The quest for freedom looms larger and larger on the horizon of modern man. It is brought more sharply into focus than ever before, perhaps because of the ever tightening grip of the machine. Vast areas of life that once were fashioned and operated by a kind of rough creativity on the part of man are now completely routinized by the machine. Leisure is becoming more and more inescapable and compulsory. Because it is compulsory, leisure is apt to be tyrannical and boring. To be able to win a span of leisure, by juggling one's responsibilities and choosing here and rejecting there, yields a certain fundamental sense of freedom for the individual. Basically, freedom is a sense of alternatives. Where there is no alternative, there is no freedom. It needs the privilege of option. Note that I say the *privilege* of option. The option need not be taken, for it may often be sufficient to know that one has an option. It is this sense of alternative that is freedom. If I had no alternative, then I could not be free. Therefore, if my freedom were perfect, absolute, it would be equivalent to slavery. Wherever human beings are denied the exercise of option, they are not free. This is confined to no particular aspect of life but is quite inclusive. "You shall know the truth and the truth shall make you free." The spirit of truth and the spirit of freedom are the same, for the truth is found only in the presence of alternatives. At long last it may be terribly accurate that paradox is the test of reality.　　— *Deep Is the Hunger,* 52–53

Once when I was very young, my grandmother, sensing the meaning of the constant threat under which I was living, told me about the message of one of the slave ministers on her plantation. Whatever he developed as his theme on the rare occasions when he was able to hold services for his fellow slaves, the climactic moment came in these exhilarating words: "You are not slaves; you are not *niggers* condemned forever to do your master's will — you are God's children." When those words were uttered a warm glow crept all through the very being of the slaves, and they felt the feeling of themselves run through them. Even at this far distance I can relive the pulsing tremor of raw energy that was released in me as I responded to her words. The sense of being permanently grounded in God gave to the people of that far-off time a way to experience themselves as human beings.

But this is one side of the coin. The community of believers must be involved in the same kind of experience. The normal reaction to experiencing oneself as a human being is to seek to experience other people as human beings. This does not have to be in the name of religion exclusively. Such a reaction is automatic unless there is some kind of intervention which short-circuits the process. The thing that determines the character of how one relates to one's fellows in any manner that has personal meaning in it, is shaped by how the individual defines others. This is but another aspect of the issue as discussed earlier. The community of Christian believers are under the judgment of a command to love God, which is the response to the awareness that God cares or loves the individual and one must love one's neighbor as oneself.

— *The Luminous Darkness*, 101–2

•

The solitariness of the human spirit, the intensely personal characteristic of all experience as distinguished from mere frustration or despair is evident in such a song as:

> I've got to walk my lonesome valley,
> I've got to walk it for myself.
> Nobody else can walk it for me,
> I've got to walk it for myself!

Here we are in the presence of an essential insight into all human experience. It seems, sometimes, that it is the solitariness of life that causes it to move with such intensity and power. In the last analysis all the great moments of profoundest meaning are solitary. We walk the ways of life together with our associates, our friends, our loved ones. How precious it is to lean upon another, to have a staggered sense of the everlasting arms felt in communion with a friend. But there are thresholds before which all must stop and no one may enter save God, and even He in disguise. I am alone but even in my aloneness I seem sometimes to be all that there is in life, and all that there is in life seems to be synthesized in me.

It is a matter of more than passing interest that this element of overwhelming poignancy is relieved somewhat by a clear note of triumph. Out of the fullness of a tremendous vitality the lowering clouds are high-lighted by an overflowing of utter exuberance:

> I feel like a motherless child;
> I feel like a motherless child;
> Glory hallelujah!
> Sometimes my way is sad and lone,
> When far away and lost from home;
> Glory hallelujah!

— *The Negro Spiritual Speaks of Life and Death,* 120

The Idol of Togetherness

"If thy soul is a stranger to thee, the whole world is unhomely."

The fight for the private life is fierce and unyielding. Often it seems as if our times are in league with the enemy. There is little rhythm of alternation between the individual and the others. Land values are so high that breathing space around the places where we live is cut away. We flee from the crowded city to the quiet of the countryside. But the countryside becomes jammed with the sounds, the noises, the sights, the pressures which were left behind. Sometimes we escape into the city from the country.

Because of the disintegration of the mood of tenderness that has overtaken us we falter in our understanding of one another. There is a certain kind of understanding abroad — it is understanding that invades, snoops, threatens, and makes afraid or embarrasses. The craftsmen of the public taste move in upon us, seeking to determine the kind of food we eat, the soap we use, the make of the car we drive, and the best way to brush our teeth. What has become of the person, the private wish?

We have made an idol of togetherness. It is the watchword of our times, it is more and more the substitute for God. In the great huddle we are desolate, lonely, and afraid. Our shoulders touch but our hearts cry out for understanding without which there can be no life and no meaning. The Great Cause, even the Cause of Survival, is not enough! There must be found ever-creative ways that can ventilate the private soul without blowing it away, that can confirm and affirm the integrity of the person in the midst of the collective necessities of our times.

There is within reach of every man a defense against the Grand Invasion. He can seek deliberately to become intimately acquainted with himself. He can cultivate an enriching life with persons, enhancing the private meaning and the personal worth. He can grow in the experience of solitude, companioned by the minds and spirits who, as Pilgrims of the Lonely Road, have left logs of their journey. He can become at home, within, by locating in his own spirit the trysting place where he and his God may meet; for it is here that life becomes *private* without being *self-centered*, that the little purposes that cloy may be absorbed in the Big Purpose that structures and redefines, that the individual comes to himself, the wanderer is home, and the private life is saved for deliberate involvement.

— *The Inward Journey,* 110–11

•

Have you ever been in a position in which you had to stand up and be counted? Really! For most of us life does not make the specifically dramatic demand of taking a formal stand. A friend of mine, a teacher in a certain divinity school, found himself in a faculty split over a special issue involving one of his colleagues and students. Eventually the board of trustees became involved in the affair. Then, one day, all members of the faculty had to take a position, for or against. To be *for,* meant to be on the side of the trustees. The issue could not be dodged;

a position had to be taken. My friend took a positive stand on an issue that was vital to him and his security, for the first time in his life. His convictions put him on the side of the minority. The next fall, he was teaching at another school. In commenting on the situation he said, "For the first time in my life, I felt that I was a man. It was the first time that I could not hedge, but instead I had to take sides in accordance with the integrity of my convictions without regard to possible consequences. I became a new person, way down deep." Of course, there are people who are always taking positions, always declaring themselves, always being counted. For such, perhaps, the dramatic character of "stand taking" is neutralized by repetition. They are professionals. There is a very important contribution made to all causes by such people. The burden of our thinking has to do with what happens when a person is pulled out of the regular routine of his life by some issue and finds himself standing up to be counted. It is a crucial experience. It means that a person is willing to take full responsibility for his actions, actions that extend beyond his little world, actions which may involve him in risk, foreign both to his temperament and to his life plan. We are living in the midst of events that make such demands upon us. The options often are very few. It is well within the possibility of the present that we shall be called upon to take a stand which will be, for us and our kind, decisive, in terms of the life and death of the person. It may not be a bad idea to get in practice now and to develop the climate within, that makes it possible for you to make up your mind — to be counted!

— Deep Is the Hunger, 7–8

A friend of mine was given an assignment in a class in dramatics. Each time she tried to read her selection aloud before the class, tears came and her strong emotional reaction made it impossible to go through with it. One day the teacher asked her to remain after class for a conference. The essence of the teacher's words to her was this: "You must read the selection before the class tomorrow. I understand what is happening to you and that is why I insist that you do this tomorrow. It is important that you realize that you must read this selection through, crying every step of the way, perhaps, if you expect to read it through without crying." A very wise teacher. There are experiences through which we must go, crying all the way, perhaps, if we are ever to go through them without crying, and to go through them without crying must be done. St. Francis of Assisi, in his youth, found it impossible to control his deep physical and emotional revulsion against leprosy. So acute was his reaction that he could not ever run the risk of looking at a leper. Shortly after he had made his first commitment to his Lord, he was riding down the road, when suddenly there appeared a leper. Instinctively, he turned his horse around and went galloping off in the opposite direction, his whole body bathed in nervous sweat. Then he realized what he was doing. Leprosy was one of the things he could not stand — as long as that was true, leprosy would be his jailer, his master. He turned around as abruptly as before, found the leper and, according to the story, remained with him, living intimately with him until every trace of his previous reaction had been mastered. Thus freed, he could be of tremendous service to the victims of the disease. You must go through some things, crying all the way, perhaps, if you are ever to live with them without crying. This is an important law of living. There are many experiences which we face that are completely overwhelming. As we see them, they are too terrible even to contemplate. And yet we must face them and deal with them directly. We chide ourselves because at first we tend to go to pieces. Go to pieces, then. Weep all the way through the first terrible impact, if need be. This may be the only way that you will ever be able to deal with the problem without emotional upheaval. To deal with it without emotional upheaval is necessary if you are ever going to be able to manage it at all. There can be no more significant personal resolution at the beginning of the New Year than this: I will face the problem I have been putting off because of too much fear, of too much tears, of too much resentment, even if it means crying all the way through, in order that I may deal with it without fear, tears, or resentment. — *Deep Is the Hunger,* 76–77

•

The need for right desire is ever present. The Apostle Paul assumes right desire when he says, "I want to do what is right, but wrong is all that I can manage." It is in order, however, to raise the question of right desire because again and again we find ourselves doing precisely only what we desire to do. Sometimes we fail to be better than we are because we do not want to be better than we are. Have you ever said, "I know I ought to want to do this or that but the truth is, I do not want to do it"? With reference to our attitude toward other people, we say sometimes, "I know I should not feel as I do toward the Germans or the Japanese or the Negroes, but the truth is, I feel that way and I really do not want to feel differently. I know that I ought to want to, but I don't." The crux of the problem is not merely that we desire the right and find it difficult to achieve it, but it is also true that, again and again, we do not desire *to desire* the right. Few questions are more searching than "Do I desire to desire the right? Do I want to do other than I am doing? Do I treat people any better than I really want to treat them?" Utter candor demands that we face questions such as these. If we find the tragedy of our lives to be that we actually do what we want to do, then, at all costs to our pride, our fears, our self-righteousness, we must change our desiring. "Teach me to desire *to desire* the right, that I may be one with Thy Will and Thy Purpose." — *Deep Is the Hunger,* 98–99

Precisely what does this [personal religious experience] mean? In the first place, he must make his choice of work, of vocation in a more restricted sense, in the light of his religious commitment. For instance, it will not be enough for him merely to be a well-trained doctor, or lawyer, or teacher. His professional training becomes a part of his total commitment to God, growing out of his religious experience. More and more his life *totally* belongs to the God of his dedication. The tools, the skills, the training, the resources of every kind which are his must be at the disposal of the commitment derived from his religious experience. The dichotomy that exists between his professional life and his private life, between his formal life and his informal life, between his inner life and his outer life, must be reduced steadily to the vanishing point. Thus wherever such a man is at work, wherever such a man is at play, there the rule of God is at hand.   — *The Creative Encounter,* 130–31

•

It is small wonder that all religions that are ethically sensitive place a great emphasis upon the corrosive effects of pride upon the human spirit. There is something very subtle about pride and arrogance of spirit. Often it assumes the garb of utter selflessness and humility. It expresses itself in pointed and dramatic self-effacement and very articulate modesty. There is often stark pride in calling attention to one's willingness always to humble oneself, to take the back seat, to accept the menial task. The most obvious basis for pride is in the act of comparing one's deeds with the deeds of others, one's achievements with the work of others. In any field of endeavor or activity, this tendency is apparent. It may be found in the comments of a parent about some other person's child, some remark made by a wife about husbands in general or a husband in particular. The idea is effectively personalized in the story which Jesus tells of the two men who went up in the temple to pray. One man said that he thanked God that he was not as other men, he paid his vows, he prayed regularly. He paused in the midst of his other duties to go into the temple to let God know how good he was. The other man, an acknowledged sinner, dared not lift his countenance to look aloft but beat at his breast asking God to be merciful to him a sinner. There is no form of pride that is quite so devastating as pride of the man who is sure that he is not victimized by pride. It is for this reason that the man who has the pride of self-righteousness can be so hard and un-yielding in dealing with others, that he can sacrifice often such feelings as tenderness, sympathy, even love, in carrying out the ruthless insistence of his autorighteous urges. The possibility of error is regarded by him as a betrayal. It must always be re-membered that the ideal is the only thing, the only standard by which one's achievements must be measured. It is fatal to measure them by the work of another man's hand or by an-other's end results. To state this in terms of religious experience, a vivid sense of the judgment of God is the only antidote to pride. That is why the holiest man is ever the one who *hon-estly* regards himself as the chief of sinners. Whatever men may think of us, however proud, righteous and decent we may be, in the eyes of God we are in some profound sense, sinners.

— *Deep Is the Hunger,* 67–68

Who, or What, is to Blame?

The desire to be one's true self is ever persistent. Equally persis-tent is the tendency to locate the responsibility for failure to be one's true self in events, persons, and conditions — all of which are outside and beyond one's self. Often a person says, "I would be the kind of person I desire to be," or "I would do the thing that I have always wanted to do *if* — ." The list is endless: if I had been born a boy rather than a girl; if I had been tall and strong rather than short and weak; if I had been given the diet

proper for a growing child; if my parents had been understanding and sympathetic rather than cold and impersonal, thereby
giving to me the feeling of being rejected; if I had lived in a different kind of community, or had grown up on the right side of
the tracks; if my parents had not separated when I was but a
child and made me the victim of a broken home; if I had not
been taught the wrong things about sex, about religion, about
myself; if I had been of a different racial or national origin —
and on and on. The interesting fact is, that in each "if" there
is apt to be, for the person who uses it, a significant element
of truth. This element of truth is seized upon as the complete
answer to the personal problem, as the single source of all the
individual's maladjustments.

There is more to the story than is indicated. Often, not
always, the person who feels most completely defeated in fulfillment is the one who has been unable or unwilling to exploit
resources that were close at hand. There is a curious inability to take personal responsibility for what one does or fails
to do, without a sense of martyrdom or heroics. Religion is
most helpful in developing in the individual a sense of personal responsibility for one's action and thus aiding the process
of self-fulfillment. It is helpful in two ways primarily: There is
the insistence upon the individual's responsibility to God for his
own life. This means that he cannot escape the scrutiny of God.
If he is responsible to God, the basis of that responsibility has
to be in himself. If it is there, then the area of alibis is definitely
circumscribed. The assumption is that the individual is ever in
immediate candidacy to get an "assist" from God — that he is
not alone in his quest. Through prayer, meditation and singleness of mind, the individual's life may be invaded by strength,
insight, and courage sufficient for his needs. Thus he need not
seek refuge in excuses but can live his life with ever-increasing
vigor and experience...an ever-deepening sense of fulfillment.

— *Meditations of the Heart*, 68–69

AT HOME IN COMMUNITY

The human spirit cannot abide the enforced loneliness of isolation. We literally feed on each other; where this nourishment is not available, the human spirit and the human body — both — sicken and die. It is not an overstatement that the purpose of all of the arrangements and conventions that make up the formal and informal agreements under which men live in society is to nourish one another *with* one another. The safeguards by which individuals or groups of men establish the boundaries of intimate and collective belonging are meant ultimately to guarantee self-nourishment. All of these are but social expressions of the underlying experience of life with itself. Life feeds on life; life is nourished by life. It is life's experience with itself that establishes the ground for the dogma that life is eternal.

To seek nourishment is a built-in urge, an ingredient of life in its simplest or most complex manifestations. The creative push that expresses itself in this way is the manner by which life realizes itself. The descriptive term that characterizes such behavior is "actualizing potential." Wherever life is observed this is its primary activity or business. In this sense all life is engaged in goal-seeking.   — *The Search for Common Ground, 3–4*

A Strange Freedom

It is a strange freedom to be adrift in the world of men without a sense of anchor anywhere. Always there is the need of mooring, the need for the firm grip on something that is rooted and will not give. The urge to be accountable to someone, to know that beyond the individual himself there is an answer that must be given, cannot be denied. The deed a man performs must be weighed in a balance held by another's hand. The very spirit of a man tends to panic from the desolation of going nameless up and down the streets of other minds where no salutation greets and no friendly recognition makes secure. It is a strange freedom to be adrift in the world of men.

Always a way must be found for bringing into one's solitary place the settled look from another's face, for getting the quiet sanction of another's grace to undergird the meaning of the self. To be ignored, to be passed over as of no account and of no meaning, is to be made into a faceless thing, not a man. It is better to be the complete victim of an anger unrestrained and a wrath which knows no bounds, to be torn asunder without mercy or battered to a pulp by angry violence, then to be passed over as if one were not. Here at least one is dealt with, encountered, vanquished, or overwhelmed — but not ignored. It is a strange freedom to go nameless up and down the streets of other minds where no salutation greets and no sign is given to mark the place one calls one's own.

The name marks the claim a man stakes against the world; it is the private banner under which he moves which is his right whatever else betides. The name is a man's water mark above which the tides can never rise. It is the thing he holds that keeps him in the way when every light has failed and every marker has been destroyed. It is the rallying point around which a man gathers all that he means by himself. It is his announcement to life that he is present and accounted for in all his parts. To be made anonymous and to give to it the acquiescence of the heart is to live without life, and for such a one, even death is no dying.

To be known, to be called by one's name, is to find one's place and hold it against all the hordes of hell. This is to *know* one's value, for one's self alone. It is to honor an act as one's very own, it is to live a life that is one's very own, it is to bow before an altar that is one's very own, it is to worship a God who is one's very own.

It is a strange freedom to be adrift in the world of men, to act with no accounting, to go nameless up and down the streets

of other minds where no salutation greets and no sign is given to mark the place one calls one's own.
— *The Inward Journey,* 37–38

The man who seeks community within his own spirit, who searches for it in his experiences with the literal facts of the external world, who makes this his formal intent as he seeks to bring order out of the chaos of his collective life, is not going against life but will be sustained and supported by life. And for the world of modern man this is crucial. In the conflicts between man and man, between group and group, between nation and nation, the loneliness of the seeker for community is sometimes unendurable. The radical tension between good and evil, as man sees it and feels it, does not have the last word about the meaning of life and the nature of existence. There is a spirit in man and in the world working always against the thing that destroys and lays waste. Always he must know that the contradictions of life are not final or ultimate; he must distinguish between failure and a many-sided awareness so that he will not mistake conformity for harmony, uniformity for synthesis. He will know that for all men to be alike is the death of life in man, and yet perceive the harmony that transcends all diversities and in which diversity finds its richness and significance.
— *The Search for Common Ground,* 6

•

The ultimate meaning of [religious] experience is felt in such a way that all of oneself is included. It is total, it is unified and unifying. It is not the experience of oneself as male or female, as black or white, as American or European. It is rather the experience of oneself as *being.* It is at such a time that one can hear the sound of the genuine in other human beings. This is to be able to identify with them. One man's response to the sound of the genuine in another man is to ascribe to the other man the same sense of infinite worth that one holds for oneself. When this happens, men are free to relate to each other as human beings — good, bad, mean, friendly, prejudiced, altruistic, but human beings. Whatever may be the nature of the shortcomings, they are seen from the view on the other side where the person lives whose shortcomings are being encountered.   *— The Luminous Darkness, 98–99*

Tidings of Destruction

We spread before Thee, our Father, all of the mounting concerns of our lives and even as we do so we are not sure of what Thou canst do about them. But there is within us the great necessity to expose the heights and the depths of our concerns to Thee, whose wisdom transcends our little wisdoms, whose caring contains all the reaches of our own love, and whose mind holds all our little minds in their place.

We are concerned as we hear the tidings of the destruction and the suffering from the raging storms and winds and the snows of winter, as in combination they beat down upon Thy children in other lands. The suffering, the desolation, the panic, the fear — these reach us even in the quietness. The concern that we feel for France and for that section of North Africa where so much violence and so much evil have been done. We try to encompass in the sweep of our awareness the intimate overtones of colossal misery and frustration and hurt and pain and hate and love. One by one we might speak of our various desires. But Thou knowest how far these reach and where they are limited and bounded by our ignorance or our indifference or by the intensity of the personal struggle with which we ourselves are faced.

We lay bare the personal concerns of our private lives: the decisions we must make and do not know how to make; the anxiety which we feel because of what is going on within our minds or our bodies, the outcome of which we cannot even guess. The little awareness of the little problems of our little lives mounts to overwhelming proportions when we still ourselves in Thy waiting presence. We ask nothing. We wait. We wait, our Father, until at last something of Thy strength becomes our strength, something of Thy heart becomes our heart, something of Thy forgiveness becomes our forgiveness. We wait, O God, we wait.   — *The Centering Moment,* 61

•

That which is innocent is essentially untried, untested, unchallenged. It is complete and whole in itself because it has known nothing else. When innocence is lost because of violation, however defined, something in the individual begins working to recover a lost grace. When the *quality* of goodness has been reestablished, a great change has taken place. Eyes are opened, knowledge is defined, and what results is the triumph of the quality of innocence over the quality of discord; a new synthesis is achieved that has in it the element of triumph. That is, a child is innocent, but a man who has learned how to winnow beauty out of ugliness, purity out of stain, tranquility out of tempest, joy out of sorrow, life out of death — only such a man may be said to be good. But he is no longer innocent....

The story of man's struggle on the planet, haunting him as he builds his cultures, his civilizations, as he erects his altars and makes his sacrifices before his God, is to find his way back to the Garden of Eden, which must yet be achieved. To achieve community in the midst of all the things he brought upon himself by his own deeds, things that work most against community, is to sweep past the angel with the flaming sword and build a new home in the Garden of Eden. At man's moments of greatest despair he is instinctively unwilling and perhaps unable to accept the contradictions of his life as final or ultimate. Something deep within reminds him that the intent of the Creator of life and the living substance is that men must live in harmony within themselves and with one another and perhaps with all of life. When he seeks to achieve it, even in his little world of belonging and meaning, what is at first the dim racial memory stirring deep within him becomes the paean of a great transcendent chorus rejoicing him on his way.

— *The Search for Common Ground*, 26–27, 27–28

It is clear that any structure of society, any arrangement under which human beings live, that does not provide maximum opportunities for free-flowing circulation among one another, works against social and individual health. Any attitudes, private or group, which prohibit people from coming into "across-the-board" contact with each other work against the implementation of the love ethic. So considered, segregation, prescriptions of separation, are a disease of the human spirit and the body politic. It does not matter how meaningful the tight circle of isolated security may be, in which individuals or groups move. The very existence of such circles, whether regarded as a necessity of religious faith, political ideology, or social purity, precludes the possibility of the experience of love as a part of the necessity of man's life.

The experience of love is either a necessity or a luxury. If it be a luxury, it is expendable; if it be a necessity, then to deny it is to perish. So simple is the reality, and so terrifying. Ultimately there is only one place of refuge on this planet for any man — that is in another man's heart. To love is to make of one's heart a swinging door.   — *Disciplines of the Spirit*, 127

NEAR JOURNEY'S END

The disintegration of human life is always difficult to handle emotionally. The wasting away in illness, the gradual fading of one's intellectual powers, the quiet ebbing of physical energy, all these are part of the disintegration of human life, with which we have to do. One watches the appearance of the first strand of gray in the hair and then, quickly or creepily, the hair blossoms with heavy frost; or the first signs of baldness, and then more and more, until one's face extends up beyond the horizon to find fulfillment in a hairy fringe on the back of the head just above the neckline; or the first crow's feet around the eyes, and then here and there a wrinkle, and then more and more, until at last the fact of ripeness of years or premature physical cracking must be dealt with fully. At such times we are apt to feel as if life is taking unfair advantage of us, stripping us of all defenses of self-respect against the world. As we watch our own powers fade, or those of our friends, we wish that life were not so tenacious. Why cannot we make a clean break of life without wasting away? It is humiliating. When such thoughts crowd into one's mind, it is good to remember that it is precisely the tenacity of life, the way in which life squeezes each solitary bit of energy out of every available source, that has made survival possible and the endurance of the "slings of outrageous fortune" within the range of the creative powers of the human spirit. Man is tough! Man's body is tough! Man's mind is tough! Again and again, the story is that man crumbles rather than crashes. (For the first time in our history, the tempo of life is so heightened that there may not be time enough to crumble, only to crash.) Life is alive and every tiny rootlet and every tiny nerve cell charged with the energy of the eternal. Old age, sickness, the fading of the powers is fought inch by inch all the way to the grave. Hallelujah!   — *Deep Is the Hunger,* 141–42

It is important then to examine this literature [the spirituals] to see what is revealed here concerning the attitude toward death. How significant is death? Is it the worst of all possible things that can happen to an individual:

Oh Freedom! Oh Freedom!
Oh Freedom, I love thee!
And before I'll be a slave,
I'll be buried in my grave,
And go home to my Lord and be free.

Obvious indeed is it here that death is not regarded as life's worst offering. There are some things in life that are worse than death. A man is not compelled to accept life without reference to the conditions upon which the offering is made. Here is something more than a mere counsel of suicide. It is a primary disclosure of an elemental affirmation having to do directly, not only with the ultimate dignity of the human spirit, but also with the ultimate basis of self-respect. We are face to face with a gross conception of the immortality of man, gross because it is completely exhaustive in its desperation. A radical conception of the immortality of man is apparent because the human spirit has a final word over the effect of circumstances. It is the guarantee of the sense of alternative in human experience, upon which, in the last analysis, all notions of freedom finally rest. Here is a recognition of death as the one fixed option which can never be taken from man by any power, however great, or by any circumstance, however fateful. If death were not implicit in the fact of life in a time-space dimension, then in no true sense would there be any authentic options in human experience: This concept regards death merely as a private option, private because it involves the single individual as if he and he alone existed in all the universe; option, because, while it assumes the inevitability of death as a factor in life, it recognizes the element of time which brings the inevitable factor under some measure of control.

The fact that death can be reduced to a manageable unit in any sense, whatsoever, reveals something that is profoundly significant concerning its character. The significant revelation is the

fact that death, as an event, is spatial, time encompassed, if not actually time bound, and therefore partakes of the character of the episodic. Death not only affects man by involving him concretely in its fulfillment, but man seems to be aware that he is being affected by death in the experience itself. There is, therefore, an element of detachment for the human spirit, even in so crucial an experience. Death is an experience in life and a man, under some circumstances, may be regarded as a spectator *of,* as well as a participant *in,* the moment of his own death. The logic here is that man is both a space binder and a time binder.
— *The Negro Spiritual Speaks of Life and Death,* 113–14

A Good Death

"I want to die easy when I die." This is a line from an old song which belonged to another period and another age. There is no gruesome note here, not a single morbid or depressing overtone. We are not face to face with something that is grim and foreboding. But we are faced with a grand conception of death that gathers in its sweep all the little fears and anxieties that condition the personal view and the private contemplation of the end of life. It is a Trumpet Call to human dignity.

The madder the world seems, the more the rumors of lethal devices reach our ears, the more we are desirous of finding and clinging to a few simple values: things that can be felt and held and owned; a bit of economic security, transitory though it be, that will give a few rare moments free of the immediate necessity of working for that day's bread; the experience of love, however fleeting, and perchance a family as a primary defense against not being wanted and not belonging. So strenuous is our pursuit for these things that it is difficult even to grasp the great concept which the line presents to the human spirit — "I want to die easy when I die."

Life and death are felt as a single respiration — the ebb and flow of a single tide. Death is not the invasion of an alien principle, it is not an attack upon life by an enemy. Death is not the Grim Reaper, the black-cowled skeleton with blazing eyes, galloping on a white horse. No! Life and death are identical twins. Therefore it is man's privilege and wisdom to make a good death, even as it is to make a good life.

A good death is made up of the same elements as a good life. A good life is what a man does with the details of living if he sees his life as an instrument, a deliberate instrument in the hands of Life, that transcends all boundaries and all horizons. It is this *beyond dimension* that saves the individual life from being swallowed by the tyranny of present needs, present hungers, and present threats. This is to put distance *within* the experience and to live the quality of the beyond even in the intensity of the present moment. And a good death — what is it? It has the same quality and character as a good life. True, the body may be stripped of all defenses by the ravages of disease; there may remain no surface expression of dignity and self-respect as the organism yields slowly to the pressure of change monitored by death. These are all secondary. The real issue is at another depth entirely. It is at the place where Life has been long since accepted and yielded to, where the private will has become infused with the Great Will, where the child of God realizes his Sonship. This is the knowledge that the son has of the Father and the Father of the son — this is to know God and to abide in Him forever.   — *The Inward Journey,* 24–25

•

All experience is raw material that goes into the making of me. Though my experiences shape me ultimately, yet I am not my experiences. I am an experiencer — but without my particular experiences I should not be what I am. I am what I am at any particular moment by standing on the shoulders of an infinite series of yesterdays. A man cannot be quite separated from his yesterdays. Modern psychology, mental healing, modern education, all take into account this basic fact. The amazing transformation of the material ideas, concepts, and ideologies of a whole nation in one generation is a case in point. It is the nature of life that we are kneaded and molded by our experience of life.

One of the profound insights of Jesus of Nazareth is that the history of a man's life is his judgment. This illustrates the point in an amazing dimension. He gives us a picture of the climax of human history in what is generally called the Great Judgment. It is a dramatic picture. The Judge, like some Oriental despot, sits enthroned. Before him come all the nations of the earth. "I was sick, you visited me. I was hungry, you fed me. I was in prison, you came unto me." Or, "I was sick and you did not visit me. I was hungry, you did not feed me. I was in prison, you did not come unto me." These are the terrible words of the Judgment. But the thing that is of tremendous import here is the fact that the Judge is merely a timekeeper, a recorder. He does not arbitrarily send a man to the right or left; it is the man's deeds that do it. The Judge is almost a figurehead — the point is made so sharply. In bold, awful outline the principle is etched in unforgettable austerity — the history of a man's life is his judgment. —*Deep River*, 73–74

RENEWAL OF THE SELF

Human Endurance

There often seems to be a clearly defined limit to human endurance. Everyone has had the experience of exhaustion. If you cannot get to bed you are sure that you will go to sleep standing. Then something happens. It may be that a friend comes by to see you, a friend whose path has not crossed yours in several years. It may be that there are tidings of good news or of tragedy. At any rate, something happens in you, with the result that you are awake, recovered, even excited. A few minutes before, the weariness was closing in like a dense fog. But now it is gone.

Of course, knowledge about the body and mind gives an increasingly satisfying explanation of this kind of experience. The important thing, however, is the fact that beyond the zero point of endurance there are vast possibilities. The precise limitations under which you live your particular life cannot be determined. Usually the stimulus, the incentive, must come from the outside — be brought to you on the wings of external circumstance. This means that the power available to you in great demand is not yours to command. I wonder!

This simple fact of revitalizing human endurance opens a great vista for living. It cannot be that what is possible to the body and nervous system by way of tapping the individual resource on demand is denied the spirit. The spirit in man is not easily vanquished. It is fragile *and* tough. You may fail again and again and yet something will not let you give up. Something keeps you from accepting "no" as a final answer. It is this quality that makes for the survival of values when the circumstances of one's life are most against decency, goodness, and right. Men tend to hold on when there seems to be no point in holding on, because they find that they *must*. It is often at such a point that the spirit in man and the spirit of God blend into one creative illumination. This is the great miracle. The body and the nervous system know.   — *The Inward Journey*, 44–45

•

There is a fallow time for the spirit when the soil is barren because of sheer exhaustion. It may come unannounced like an overnight visitor "passing through." It may be sudden as a sharp turn-in on an unfamiliar road. It may come at the end of a long, long period of strenuous effort in handling some slippery in-and-out temptation that fails to follow a pattern. It may result from the plateau of tragedy that quietly wore away the growing edge of alertness until nothing was left but the exhausted roots of aliveness. The general climate of social unrest, of national and international turmoil, the falling of kingdoms, the constant, muted suffering of hungry men and starving women and children on the other sides of the oceans, all these things may so paralyze normal responses to life that a blight settles over the spirit leaving all the fields of interest withered and parched. It is quite possible that spreading oneself so thin with too much going "to and fro" has yielded a fever of activity that saps all energy, even from one's surplus store, and we must stop for the quiet replenishing of an empty cupboard. Perhaps too much anxiety, a too-hard trying, a searching strain to do by oneself what can never be done that way, has made one's spirit seem like a water tap whose washer is worn out from too much pressure. But withal there may be the simplest possible explanation: the rhythmic ebb and flow of one's powers, simply this and nothing more. Whatever may be the reasons, one has to deal with the fact. Face it! Then resolutely dig out dead roots, clear the ground, but don't forget to make a humus pit against the time when some young or feeble plants will need stimulation from past flowerings in your garden. Work out new designs by dreaming daring dreams and great and creative planning. The time is not wasted. The time of fallowness is a time of rest and restoration, of filling up and replenishing. It is the moment when the meaning of all things can be searched out, tracked down, and made to yield the secret of living. Thank God for the fallow time!   — *Deep Is the Hunger,* 89–90

The Night View of the World

"Upon the night view of the world, a day view must follow." This is an ancient insight grounded in the experience of the race in its long journey through all the years of man's becoming. Here is no cold idea born out of the vigil of some solitary thinker in lonely retreat from the traffic of the common ways. It is not the wisdom of the book put down in ordered words by the learned and the schooled. It is insight woven into the pattern of all living things, reaching its grand apotheosis in the reflection of man gazing deep into the heart of his own experience.

That the day view follows the night view is written large in nature. Indeed it is one with nature itself. The clouds gather heavy with unshed tears; at last they burst, sending over the total landscape waters gathered from the silent offering of sea and river. The next day dawns and the whole heavens are aflame with the glorious brilliance of the sun. This is the way the rhythm moves. The fall of the year comes, then winter with its trees stripped of leaf and bud; cold winds ruthless in bitterness and sting. One day there is sleet and ice; in the silence of the nighttime the snow falls soundlessly — all this until at last the cold seems endless and all there is seems to be shadowy and foreboding. The earth is weary and heavy. Then something stirs — a strange new vitality pulses through everything. One can feel the pressure of some vast energy pushing, always pushing through dead branches, slumbering roots — life surges everywhere within and without. Spring has come. The day usurps the night view.

Is there any wonder that deeper than idea and concept is the insistent conviction that the night can never stay, that winter is ever moving toward the spring? Thus, when a man sees the lights go out one by one, when he sees the end of his days marked by death — his death — he *senses,* rather than knows, that even the night into which he is entering will be followed by day. It remains for religion to give this ancient wisdom phrase and symbol. For millions of men and women in many climes this phrase and this symbol are forever one with Jesus, the

Prophet from Galilee. When the preacher says as a part of the last rites, "I am the Resurrection and the Life, . . . " he is reminding us all of the ancient wisdom: "Upon the night view of the world, a day view must follow."

— *The Inward Journey,* 47–48

Life Goes On

During these turbulent times we must remind ourselves repeatedly that life goes on. This we are apt to forget. The wisdom of life transcends our wisdoms; the purpose of life outlasts our purposes; the process of life cushions our processes. The mass attack of disillusion and despair, distilled out of the collapse of hope, has so invaded our thoughts that what we know to be true and valid seems unreal and ephemeral. There seems to be little energy left for aught but futility. This is the great deception. By it whole peoples have gone down to oblivion without the will to affirm the great and permanent strength of the clean and the commonplace. Let us not be deceived. It is just as important as ever to attend to the little graces by which the dignity of our lives is maintained and sustained. Birds still sing; the stars continue to cast their gentle gleam over the desolation of the battlefields, and the heart is still inspired by the kind word and the gracious deed. There is no need to fear evil. There is every need to understand what it does, how it operates in the world, what it draws upon to sustain itself. We must not shrink from the knowledge of the evilness of evil. Over and over we must know that the real target of evil is not destruction of the body, the reduction to rubble of cities; the real target of evil is to corrupt the spirit of man and to give to his soul the contagion of inner disintegration. When this happens, there is nothing left, the very citadel of man is captured and laid waste. Therefore the evil in the world around us must not be allowed to move from without to within. This would be to be overcome by evil. To drink in the beauty that is within reach, to clothe one's life with simple deeds of kindness, to keep alive a sensitiveness to the movement of the spirit of God in the quietness of the human heart and in the workings of the human mind — this is as always the ultimate answer to the great deception.

— *The Meditations of the Heart,* 110–11

•

There must be always remaining in every man's life some place for the singing of angels, some place for that which in itself is breathlessly beautiful and, by an inherent prerogative, throws all the rest of life into a new and creative relatedness, something that gathers up in itself all the freshets of experience from drab and commonplace areas of living and glows in one bright white light of penetrating beauty and meaning — then passes. The commonplace is shot through with new glory; old burdens become lighter; deep and ancient wounds lose much of their old, old hurting. A crown is placed over our heads that for the rest of our lives we are trying to grow tall enough to wear. Despite all the crassness of life, despite all the hardness of life, despite all the harsh discords of life, life is saved by the singing angels.

— *Deep Is the Hunger,* 91–92

Keep Alive the Dream in the Heart

As long as a man has a dream in his heart, he cannot lose the significance of living. It is a part of the pretensions of modern life to traffic in what is generally called "realism." There is much insistence upon being practical, down to earth. Such things as dreams are wont to be regarded as romantic or as a badge of immaturity, or as escape hatches for the human spirit. When such a mood or attitude is carefully scrutinized, it is found to be made up largely of pretensions, in short, of bluff. Men cannot continue long to live if the dream in the heart has perished. It is then that they stop hoping, stop looking, and the last embers of their anticipations fade away.

The dream in the heart is the outlet. It is one with the living water welling up from the very springs of Being, nourishing and sustaining all of life. Where there is no dream, the life becomes a swamp, a dreary dead place and, deep within, a man's heart begins to rot. The dream need not be some great and overwhelming plan; it need not be a dramatic picture of what might or must be someday; it need not be a concrete outpouring of a world-shaking possibility of sure fulfillment. Such may be important for some; such may be crucial for a particular moment of human history. But it is not in these grand ways that the dream nourishes life. The dream is the quiet persistence in the heart that enables a man to ride out the storms of his churning experiences. It is the exciting whisper moving through the aisles of his spirit answering the monotony of limitless days of dull routine. It is the ever-recurring melody in the midst of the broken harmony and harsh discords of human conflict. It is the touch of significance which highlights the ordinary experience, the common event. The dream is no outward thing. It does not take its rise from the environment in which one moves or functions. It lives in the inward parts, it is deep within, where the issues of life and death are ultimately determined. Keep alive the dream; for as long as a man has a dream in his heart, he cannot lose the significance of living.

— *Meditations of the Heart,* 36–37

I Will Sing a New Song

The old song of my spirit has wearied itself out.
It has long ago been learned by heart;
It repeats itself over and over,
Bringing no added joy to my day or lift to my spirit.

I will sing a new song.
I must learn the new song for the new needs.
I must fashion new words born of all the new growth
    of my life — of my mind — of my spirit.
I must prepare for new melodies that have
    never been mine before,
That all that is within me may lift my voice unto God.
Therefore, I shall rejoice with each new day
And delight my spirit in each fresh unfolding.
I will sing, this day, a new song unto the Lord.

— *The Mood of Christmas*, 24

The Growing Edge

Look well to the growing edge. All around us worlds are dying
and new worlds are being born; all around us life is dying and
life is being born. The fruit ripens on the tree, the roots are
silently at work in the darkness of the earth against a time when
there shall be new leaves, fresh blossoms, green fruit. Such is the
growing edge! It is the extra breath from the exhausted lung,
the one more thing to try when all else has failed, the upward
reach of life when weariness closes in upon all endeavor. This is
the basis of hope in moments of despair, the incentive to carry
on when times are out of joint and men have lost their reason,
the source of confidence when worlds crash and dreams whiten
into ash. The birth of the child — life's most dramatic answer
to death — this is the growing edge incarnate. Look well to the
growing edge!   — *Meditations of the Heart*, 134